Cisneros

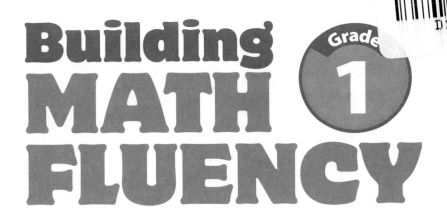

Building MATH FLUENCY

Grade **1**

D1027039

Consultant: Eleanor Falk Young
Editorial Development: Joy Evans
Jo Ellen Moore
Copy Editing: Carrie Gwynne
Art Direction: Cheryl Puckett
Cover Design: Liliana Potigian
Illustration: Jo Larsen
Design/Production: Marcia Smith

EMC 3033

Evan-Moor
EDUCATIONAL PUBLISHERS
Helping Children Learn since 1979

Congratulations on your purchase of some of the finest teaching materials in the world.

For information about other Evan-Moor products, call 1-800-777-4362, fax 1-800-777-4332, or visit our Web site, www.evan-moor.com.
Entire contents © 2008 EVAN-MOOR CORP.
18 Lower Ragsdale Drive, Monterey, CA 93940-5746. Printed in USA.

Correlated to State Standards

Visit *teaching-standards.com* to view a correlation of this book's activities to your state's standards. This is a free service.

CPSIA: Printed by McNaughton & Gunn, Saline, MI USA. [2/2011]:Book
CPSIA: Lehigh Phoenix, 8111 North 87th St., Milwaukee, WI USA. 53224 [2/2011]:Transparencies

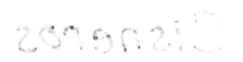

Contents

Addition Tests

Subtraction Tests

Student Practice Flashcards

Answer Key

Transparencies

What's in This Book?

Mathematics standards frequently contain terminology such as "numerical fluency," "computational accuracy," and "automaticity." These terms recognize that the ability to compute quickly and accurately aids in higher-level mathematics and problem solving.

The goal of *Building Math Fluency* is to provide students with tools for thinking about computation in logical, strategic ways. Mastery of math facts is facilitated by understanding number relationships. Mastery is further enhanced with sufficient practice.

Strategy Practice

There is a section of strategy practice for each operation presented in this book. These practice pages can be done with students in a whole class or in small groups. Students benefit when teachers and peers model the use of the strategies and verbalize solution strategies aloud.

Charts of the strategies are presented both as reproducibles and as transparencies at the back of this book.

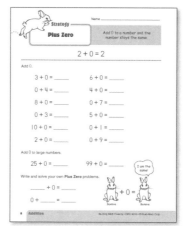

Practice pages feature a strategy box and problems to solve using that strategy.

Test Your Skills

The *Test Your Skills* pages provide concentrated fact practice. These pages can be used in a number of ways, as described on page 76. A feature of *Test Your Skills* is the opportunity for students to evaluate their own performance.

Facts Flashcards

Reproducible flashcards for the operations covered in this book are provided. The teacher resource page at the beginning of the section gives suggestions for using the cards to enhance students' mastery of number facts.

Glossary of Mathematics Terms

Addends The numbers in an addition problem.

$$3 + 4 = 7 \leftarrow \text{sum}$$
$$\underset{\text{addend}}{\uparrow} \quad \uparrow$$

Commutative Property of Addition Numbers can be added in any order without changing the sum.

$$3 + 4 = 7 \qquad 4 + 3 = 7$$

Difference The result of subtracting two numbers.

$$16 - 7 = \underset{\text{difference}}{9}$$

Digit Any of the symbols 0, 1, 2, 3, 4, 5, 6, 7, 8, 9 used to write a number.

Fact Family A group of related facts, either addition or subtraction.

$$8 + 4 = 12 \qquad 4 + 8 = 12 \qquad 12 - 4 = 8 \qquad 12 - 8 = 4$$

Identity Property of Addition When 0 is added to a number, it does not change the total.

Minuend The number being subtracted from.

$$\underset{\text{minuend}}{16} - 7 = 9$$

Place Value The value of a digit as determined by its position in the ones place, tens place, and so forth. Each position is ten times of the place to its right and one-tenth of the place to its left.

Subtrahend The number being subtracted.

$$16 - \underset{\text{subtrahend}}{7} = 9$$

Sum The result of joining quantities; the total.

$$3 + 4 = \underset{\text{sum}}{7}$$

Teaching Addition Strategies

Pages 8–44 present practice with addition strategies that promote computational fluency and fact mastery.

Plus Zero means add 0 to any number and the number stays the same.

$3 + 0 = 3$

Count Up is a strategy to use when adding a small number (1, 2, or 3) to a larger quantity. Students start with the larger addend and count up the smaller addend to find the total.

Turn Around means that the order of the addends does not change the total.

$4 + 1 = 5$ and $1 + 4 = 5$

Doubles are facts in which an addend is added to itself. Students often discover that Doubles are always even numbers. When students have learned the Doubles facts, they have an "anchor" from which to compute many other facts.

$1 + 1 = 2$	$3 + 3 = 6$	$5 + 5 = 10$	$7 + 7 = 14$	$9 + 9 = 18$
$2 + 2 = 4$	$4 + 4 = 8$	$6 + 6 = 12$	$8 + 8 = 16$	$10 + 10 = 20$

Doubles Plus One means double the number and add one more.

$6 + 6 = 12$ becomes $6 + 6 + 1 = 13$ and that means $6 + 7 = 13$

Tens Partners are number pairs that make 10.

$0 + 10 = 10$	$2 + 8 = 10$	$4 + 6 = 10$
$1 + 9 = 10$	$3 + 7 = 10$	$5 + 5 = 10$

Plus Ten means that when 10 is added to a number, the tens-place digit increases by one, while the ones-place digit stays the same.

$30 + 10 = 40$ $40 + 10 = 50$

Addition Strategies

Plus Zero	Add 0 to a number and the number stays the same. $3 + 0 = 3$
Count Up $+1, +2, +3$	Count Up when adding on small numbers, such as 1, 2, or 3.
Turn Around	Add numbers in any order and the total stays the same. $3 + 1 = 4 \qquad 1 + 3 = 4$
Doubles	Add the number to itself and that number doubles. $2 + 2 = 4$
Doubles Plus One and minus one	Double the number and add one more. $2 + 3 = 2 + 2 + 1$
Tens Partners	There are six sets of number pairs that make 10: $10 + 0 \quad 9 + 1 \quad 8 + 2$ $7 + 3 \quad 6 + 4 \quad 5 + 5$
Plus Ten	When 10 is added to a number, the tens-place digit increases by one. $30 + 10 = 40$

Strategy

Plus Zero

Add 0 to a number and the number stays the same.

$$2 + 0 = 2$$

Add 0.

$3 + 0 =$ _____ $6 + 0 =$ _____

$0 + 4 =$ _____ $4 + 0 =$ _____

$8 + 0 =$ _____ $0 + 7 =$ _____

$0 + 3 =$ _____ $5 + 0 =$ _____

$10 + 0 =$ _____ $0 + 1 =$ _____

$2 + 0 =$ _____ $0 + 9 =$ _____

Add 0 to large numbers.

$25 + 0 =$ _____ $99 + 0 =$ _____

Write and solve your own **Plus Zero** problems.

_____ $+ 0 =$ _____

$0 +$ _____ $=$ _____

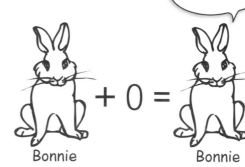

I am the same!

Bonnie + 0 = Bonnie

Strategy
Count Up
+1, +2, +3

Count Up when adding on
small numbers, such as 1, 2, or 3.

To solve 3 + 2, start at 3. Circle 3.
Count up 2 hops. Underline the answer.

$$3 + 2 = 5$$

Add. Use the **Count Up** strategy.
Show your hops on the number line.

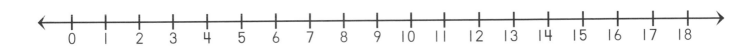

4 + 1 = _____

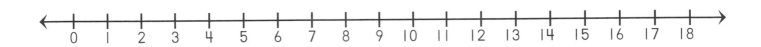

6 + 2 = _____

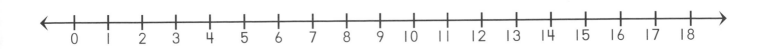

4 + 3 = _____

Strategy

Count Up
+1, +2, +3

Count Up when adding on small numbers, such as 1, 2, or 3.

Find the sums.
Use the number lines.

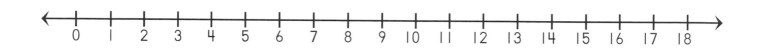

2 + 1 = _____   5 + 2 = _____   9 + 3 = _____

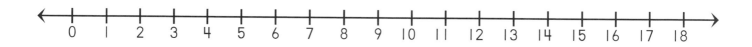

1 + 1 = _____   3 + 2 = _____   8 + 3 = _____

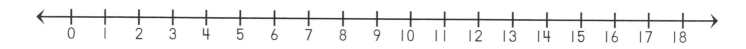

4 + 1 = _____   7 + 2 = _____   11 + 3 = _____

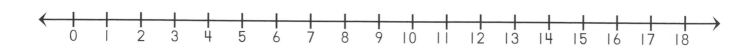

3 + 1 = _____   8 + 2 = _____   14 + 3 = _____

Count Up
+1, +2, +3

Name _____

Count Up when adding on
small numbers, such as 1, 2, or 3.

$$4 + 2 = \underline{6}$$

Solve the problems.
Use the number line.

$5 + 2 = \underline{\hspace{2cm}}$ $3 + 2 = \underline{\hspace{2cm}}$

$6 + 1 = \underline{\hspace{2cm}}$ $8 + 3 = \underline{\hspace{2cm}}$

$9 + 1 = \underline{\hspace{2cm}}$ $4 + 3 = \underline{\hspace{2cm}}$

8	15	7
+ 1	+ 3	+ 2

9	10	8
+ 3	+ 1	+ 2

18
17
16
15
14
13
12
11
10
9
8
7
6
5
4
3
2
1
0

Strategy

Count Up
+1, +2, +3

Count Up when adding on
small numbers, such as 1, 2, or 3.

$$6 + \boxed{2} = 8$$

Count how many jumps you need to get to the answer.

$3 + \boxed{} = 5$ $4 + \boxed{} = 7$

$9 + \boxed{} = 10$ $6 + \boxed{} = 9$

$7 + \boxed{} = 8$ $2 + \boxed{} = 3$

$9 + \boxed{} = 12$ $8 + \boxed{} = 11$

$7 + \boxed{} = 9$ $13 + \boxed{} = 15$

Try it this way.

$$\begin{array}{r} 5 \\ + \boxed{} \\ \hline 6 \end{array} \qquad \begin{array}{r} 6 \\ + \boxed{} \\ \hline 8 \end{array} \qquad \begin{array}{r} 3 \\ + \boxed{} \\ \hline 6 \end{array}$$

17
16
15
14
13
12
11
10
9
8
7
6
5
4
3
2
1
0

12   **Addition**

Building Math Fluency • EMC 3033 • © Evan-Moor Corp.

Strategy
Count Up
+1, +2, +3

Count Up when adding on small numbers, such as 1, 2, or 3.

Use the number line to help you count.

3 + ☐ = 6

8 + ☐ = 9

3 + 2 = ☐

6 + ☐ = 8

7 + ☐ = 9

5 + ☐ = 7

6 + 3 = ☐

10 + ☐ = 11

5 + 3 = ☐

14 + 2 = ☐

17
16
15
14
13
12
11
10
9
8
7
6
5
4
3
2
1
0

Write and solve your own **Count Up** problems.

☐ + 1 = ☐

☐ + 2 = ☐

☐ + 3 = ☐

Strategy

Count Up
+1, +2, +3

Name _____

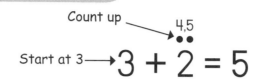

Count up → 4,5
• •

Start at 3 → $3 + 2 = 5$

Draw dots.
Count Up.

5,6,7
• • •
$4 + 3 = \underline{}$

7,8
• •
$6 + 2 = \underline{}$

$6 + 1 = \underline{}$

$7 + 3 = \underline{}$

$8 + 3 = \underline{}$

$5 + 1 = \underline{}$

$9 + 2 = \underline{}$

$10 + 3 = \underline{}$

$7 + 1 = \underline{}$

$4 + 2 = \underline{}$

$6 + 3 = \underline{}$

$10 + 2 = \underline{}$

Building Math Fluency • EMC 3033 • © Evan-Moor Corp.

Strategy
Count Up
+1, +2, +3

Count Up when adding on
small numbers, such as 1, 2, or 3.

Circle the greater number.
This is the largest *addend*.
Count Up from the largest addend.

7,8,9
• • •
3 + ⑥ = _____ 9

9,10
• •
⑧ + 2 = _____

7 + 3 = _____

5 + 2 = _____

9 + 3 = _____

7 + 2 = _____

6 + 2 = _____

1 + 5 = _____

3 + 4 = _____

2 + 6 = _____

1 + 14 = _____

3 + 10 = _____

11 + 1 = _____

3 + 12 = _____

Strategy

Count Up

+1, +2, +3

Count Up when adding on
small numbers, such as 1, 2, or 3.

Find the sums.

$$9 + 3$$

$$3 + 10 =$$

$$5 + 3$$

$$13 + 3 =$$

$$7 + 3 =$$

$$16 + 2$$

$$2 + 9$$

$$20 + 3 =$$

$$15 + 1$$

Think about how you solved the problems. Mark **yes** or **no**.

Did you:

		yes	no
draw dots to count up?	$13 + \overset{\cdots}{3}$	☐	☐
count up from the larger number?	$⑬ + 3$	☐	☐
use a number line?	←─┼─┼─┼─┼─→ 13 14 15 16	☐	☐

Strategy
Turn Around

Add numbers in any order and the total stays the same.

When you learn one addition fact, you really learn two.

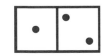

__1__ + __2__ = __3__   turn around   __2__ + __1__ = __3__

____ + ____ = ____   turn around   ____ + ____ = ____

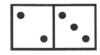

____ + ____ = ____   turn around   ____ + ____ = ____

Write the **Turn Around** fact.

1 + 3 = ____ + ____   4 + 5 = ____ + ____

2 + 4 = ____ + ____   9 + 2 = ____ + ____

8 + 1 = ____ + ____   5 + 7 = ____ + ____

Doubles

Name _____

Add the number to itself and
that number doubles.

Solve the **Doubles** facts.

__2__ + __2__ = __4__

_____ + _____ = _____

_____ + _____ = _____

_____ + _____ = _____

_____ + _____ = _____

_____ + _____ = _____

_____ + _____ = _____

Building Math Fluency • EMC 3033 • © Evan-Moor Corp.

Name _____

Strategy

Doubles

Match the picture with the fact.

• 3 + 3 = _____

• 8 + 8 = _____

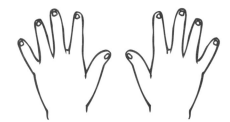

• 6 + 6 = _____

• 5 + 5 = _____

• 4 + 4 = _____

Strategy

Doubles

Add the number to itself and
that number doubles.

Draw dots to complete the double dominoes.
Solve the **Doubles** facts.

$1 + \underline{1} = \underline{2}$

$3 + \underline{3} = \underline{}$

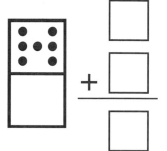

$\underline{} + \underline{} = \underline{}$

$\underline{} + \underline{} = \underline{}$

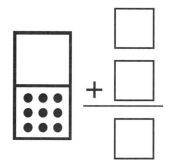

$\underline{} + \underline{} = \underline{}$

$\underline{} + \underline{} = \underline{}$

Complete the domino with **Doubles**. Solve the Doubles fact.

$\underline{} + \underline{} = 8$

$\underline{} + \underline{} = 10$

Strategy

Doubles

Add the number to itself and that number doubles.

Make tally marks to help you find the sum. Complete the chart.

Doubles Fact	Tally Marks	Sum
1 + 1	¦ + ¦	2
2 + 2		
3 + 3		
4 + 4		
5 + 5		
6 + 6	⊬⊥⊤ ¦ + ⊬⊥⊤ ¦	
7 + 7		
8 + 8		
9 + 9		
10 + 10		

Strategy

Doubles Plus One

Name _____

Double the number and add one more.

Double the number. Add one more.

3 ○○○   3 ○○○
+ 3 ○○○      + 4 ○○○●
___   ___
6   7

Solve the problems.

Doubles		Doubles + 1

4 ○○○○   4 ○○○○
+ 4 ○○○○      + 5 ○○○○●
____   ____

5 ○○○○○   5 ○○○○○
+ 5 ○○○○○   + 6 ○○○○○●
____   ____

6 ○○○○○○   6 ○○○○○○
+ 6 ○○○○○○   + 7 ○○○○○○●
____   ____

7 ○○○○○○○   7 ○○○○○○○
+ 7 ○○○○○○○   + 8 ○○○○○○○●
____   ____

Strategy

Doubles Plus One

Double the number and add one more.

Solve the **Doubles** fact.
Then add a dot to solve the **Doubles Plus One** fact.

Doubles	Doubles + 1

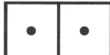 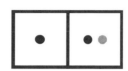

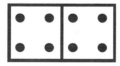 + ___ = ___   = ___

$\_\_\_ + \_\_\_ = \_\_\_$ $\_\_\_ + \_\_\_ = \_\_\_$

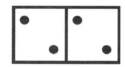 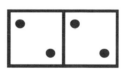

$\_\_\_ + \_\_\_ = \_\_\_$ $\_\_\_ + \_\_\_ = \_\_\_$

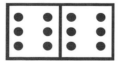 

$\_\_\_ + \_\_\_ = \_\_\_$ $\_\_\_ + \_\_\_ = \_\_\_$

$\_\_\_ + \_\_\_ = \_\_\_$ $\_\_\_ + \_\_\_ = \_\_\_$

Strategy

Doubles Plus One

Name _____

Double the number and add one more.

Complete the number equations.

Doubles		Doubles + 1
2 + 2 = __4__	so	2 + 3 = __5__
3 + 3 = _____	so	3 + 4 = _____
4 + 4 = _____	so	4 + 5 = _____
5 + 5 = _____	so	5 + 6 = _____
6 + 6 = _____	so	6 + 7 = _____
7 + 7 = _____	so	7 + 8 = _____
8 + 8 = _____	so	8 + 9 = _____
9 + 9 = _____	so	9 + 10 = _____

Building Math Fluency • EMC 3033 • © Evan-Moor Corp.

Strategy

Doubles Plus One

Double the number and add one more.

Solve and match.
Each **Doubles** fact has two **Doubles Plus One** facts.

Doubles Facts

2 + 2 = _____

3 + 3 = _____

4 + 4 = _____

5 + 5 = _____

6 + 6 = _____

7 + 7 = _____

Doubles + 1 Facts

3 + 4 = _____
4 + 3 = _____

2 + 3 = _____
3 + 2 = _____

5 + 6 = _____
6 + 5 = _____

6 + 7 = _____
7 + 6 = _____

4 + 5 = _____
5 + 4 = _____

7 + 8 = _____
8 + 7 = _____

Strategy
Tens Partners

Number pairs that make 10 are called **Tens Partners**.

Color the boxes to show **Tens Partners** combinations.
Use red for the first number and yellow for the second number.

9 + 1 = 10

red	red	red	red	red	red	red	red	red	yellow

8 + 2 = 10

7 + 3 = 10

6 + 4 = 10

5 + 5 = 10

4 + 6 = 10

3 + 7 = 10

2 + 8 = 10

1 + 9 = 10

Building Math Fluency • EMC 3033 • © Evan-Moor Corp.

Strategy

Tens Partners

Number pairs that make 10 are called **Tens Partners**.

Complete the equations. Color the boxes to show **Tens Partners** in each row. Use blue and red.

Color blue ↓   Color red ↓

	blue	red	red	red	red	red	red	red	red	red	
1 + 9											= 10
2 + 8											= 10
3 + ___											= 10
4 + ___											= 10
5 + ___											= 10
6 + ___											= 10
7 + ___											= 10
8 + ___											= 10
9 + ___											= 10
___ + 0											= 10

Strategy

Tens Partners

Count the dark and light circles in each ten frame.
Record the combinations of 10.

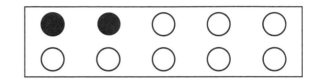

$\underline{1} + \underline{9} = 10$

●   ○

$\underline{} + \underline{} = 10$

●   ○

$\underline{} + \underline{} = \underline{}$

●   ○

$\underline{} + \underline{} = \underline{}$

●   ○

$\underline{} + \underline{} = \underline{}$

●   ○

$\underline{} + \underline{} = \underline{}$

●   ○

Complete the **Turn Around** facts.

$8 + 2 = 10$ and $\underline{2 + 8 = 10}$ $6 + 4 = 10$ and $\underline{}$

Strategy

Tens Partners

Number pairs that make 10 are called **Tens Partners**.

Follow the directions. Complete the equations.

Color 2 radishes **red**.
Color the others **yellow**.

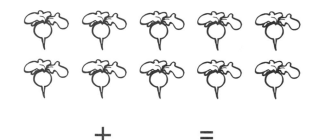

_____ + _____ = _____

Color 6 radishes **red**.
Color the others **yellow**.

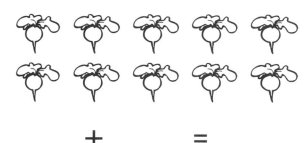

_____ + _____ = _____

Color 5 radishes **red**.
Color the others **yellow**.

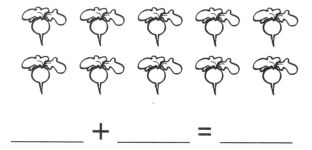

_____ + _____ = _____

Color 3 radishes **red**.
Color the others **yellow**.

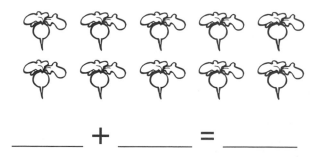

_____ + _____ = _____

Color 9 radishes **red**.
Color the others **yellow**.

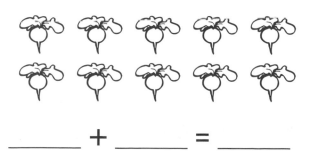

_____ + _____ = _____

Color _____ radishes **red**.
Color the others **yellow**.

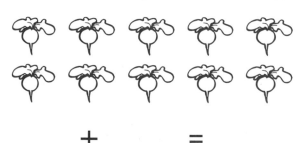

_____ + _____ = _____

Strategy

Tens Partners

Number pairs that make 10
are called **Tens Partners**.

This is a set of 10.

How many fingers are up? How many fingers are down?

___7___ + ___3___ = 10
  up   down

_____ + _____ = 10
  up   down

_____ + _____ = 10
  up   down

_____ + _____ = 10
  up   down

_____ + _____ = 10
  up   down

_____ + _____ = 10
  up   down

Strategy

Tens Partners

Name _____

Number pairs that make 10 are called **Tens Partners**.

Solve.

$9 + \boxed{} = 10$ $7 + 3 = \boxed{}$ $5 + \boxed{} = 10$

$\begin{array}{r} 8 \\ + \boxed{} \\ \hline 10 \end{array}$ $\begin{array}{r} 6 \\ + \boxed{} \\ \hline 10 \end{array}$ $\begin{array}{r} 1 \\ + \boxed{} \\ \hline 10 \end{array}$ $\begin{array}{r} 4 \\ + \boxed{} \\ \hline 10 \end{array}$

Circle the **Tens Partners**.

8 and 2   9 and 3   4 and 5

7 and 2   1 and 9   10 and 0

5 and 5   6 and 4   7 and 3

6 and 2   9 and 2   4 and 6

Do you know the number pairs that make 10?

Strategy

Plus Ten

When 10 is added to a number, the tens-place digit increases by one.

Start at 2 and jump up 10.

$2 + 10 =$ _12_

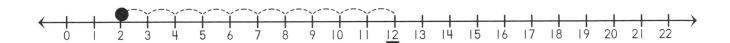

Start at 3 and jump up 10.

$3 + 10 =$ _____

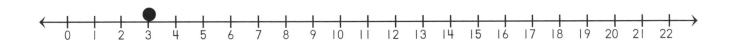

Start at 4 and jump up 10.

$4 + 10 =$ _____

Complete the chart.

Number	Number + 10
2	12
3	
4	
5	

Building Math Fluency • EMC 3033 • © Evan-Moor Corp.

Strategy

Plus Ten

When 10 is added to a number, the tens-place digit increases by one.

Add 10 to each number. Jump up on the number grid.

a Shade the number 2.
Start at 2 and add 10.
Shade where you land.

2 + 10 = _____

b Shade the number 12.
Start at 12 and add 10.
Shade where you land.

12 + 10 = _____

c Shade the number 4.
Start at 4 and add 10.
Shade where you land.

4 + 10 = _____

d Shade the number 14.
Start at 14 and add 10.
Shade where you land.

14 + 10 = _____

e Shade the number 17.
Start at 17 and add 10.
Shade where you land.

17 + 10 = _____

f Shade the number 27.
Start at 27 and add 10.
Shade where you land.

27 + 10 = _____

1	2	3	4	5	6	7	8	9	10
11	12	13	14	15	16	17	18	19	20
21	22	23	24	25	26	27	28	29	30
31	32	33	34	35	36	37	38	39	40

Strategy

Plus Ten

When 10 is added to a number, the tens-place digit increases by one.

Add 10 each time.
Solve with the number grid.

$2 + 10 =$ _____

$7 + 10 =$ _____

$3 + 10 =$ _____

$8 + 10 =$ _____

$4 + 10 =$ _____

$9 + 10 =$ _____

$5 + 10 =$ _____

$12 + 10 =$ _____

$6 + 10 =$ _____

$23 + 10 =$ _____

1	2	3	4	5	6	7	8	9	10
11	12	13	14	15	16	17	18	19	20
21	22	23	24	25	26	27	28	29	30
31	32	33	34	35	36	37	38	39	40

Strategy

Plus Ten

Jump 10. It's faster than counting by ones.

$$2 + 10 = \underline{12}$$

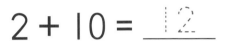

Jump 10 each time. Use the number line to solve.

$$7 + 10 = \underline{}$$

$$13 + 10 = \underline{}$$

$$19 + 10 = \underline{}$$

Write and solve your own problem. Show it on the number line.

$$\underline{} + 10 = \underline{}$$

Strategy

Plus Ten

When 10 is added to a number, the tens-place digit increases by one.

Add 10 to each number. Fill in the chart.

Number	Number + 10
3	13
4	
5	
6	
7	
	18
	19
10	
11	
	22
13	
14	

Number	Number + 10
15	
16	
	27
18	
	29
20	
30	
40	
50	
60	
70	
80	

Note: You may want to provide a number grid or number line to help students complete the chart.

Building Math Fluency • EMC 3033 • © Evan-Moor Corp.

Name _____

Doubles and More

Circle the **Doubles** facts.
Then solve the problems.

$$\begin{array}{r} 4 \\ +\ 4 \\ \hline 8 \end{array} \qquad \begin{array}{r} 8 \\ +\ 1 \\ \hline \end{array} \qquad \begin{array}{r} 5 \\ +\ 5 \\ \hline \end{array} \qquad \begin{array}{r} 5 \\ +\ 6 \\ \hline \end{array}$$

$$\begin{array}{r} 2 \\ +\ 8 \\ \hline \end{array} \qquad \begin{array}{r} 7 \\ +\ 7 \\ \hline \end{array} \qquad \begin{array}{r} 2 \\ +\ 2 \\ \hline \end{array} \qquad \begin{array}{r} 3 \\ +\ 3 \\ \hline \end{array}$$

$$\begin{array}{r} 6 \\ +\ 6 \\ \hline \end{array} \qquad \begin{array}{r} 8 \\ +\ 8 \\ \hline \end{array} \qquad \begin{array}{r} 7 \\ +\ 3 \\ \hline \end{array} \qquad \begin{array}{r} 9 \\ +\ 9 \\ \hline \end{array}$$

Think about **Doubles**. Solve the problems.

$1 + 1 =$ _____ $\qquad\qquad$ $10 + 10 =$ _____

$2 + 2 =$ _____ $\qquad\qquad$ $20 + 20 =$ _____

$3 + 3 =$ _____ $\qquad\qquad$ $30 + 30 =$ _____

Mixed Strategies Practice

Name _____

Which Strategy Fits?

Cut and glue the facts under the best strategy.

Plus Zero Add 0 to a number and the number stays the same.	**Count Up** +1, +2, +3 Count up from the larger number. Add on 1, 2, or 3.

✂

$7 + 1$	$0 + 5$	$6 + 2$
$6 + 0$	$4 + 3$	$8 + 0$
$5 + 2$	$0 + 3$	

Mixed Strategies Practice

Name _____

Which Strategy Fits?

Cut and glue the facts under the best strategy.

Doubles Add the number to itself.	**Doubles Plus One** Double the number. Add one more.

✂ -

5 + 6	9 + 9	4 + 4
3 + 4	8 + 9	5 + 5
4 + 5	8 + 8	

Mixed Strategies Practice

Name _____

Color Fun

Solve the **Plus Zero** and **Count Up** +1, +2, +3 facts on the addition chart. Shade the boxes with the correct color.

> **Plus Zero**—yellow   **Count Up** +1, +2, +3—red

+	0	1	2	3	4	5	6	7	8	9	10
0	0+0	0+1	0+2	0+3	0+4	0+5	0+6	0+7	0+8	0+9	0+10
1	1+0	1+1	1+2	1+3	1+4	1+5	1+6	1+7	1+8	1+9	1+10
2	2+0	2+1	2+2	2+3	2+4	2+5	2+6	2+7	2+8	2+9	2+10
3	3+0	3+1	3+2	3+3	3+4	3+5	3+6	3+7	3+8	3+9	3+10
4	4+0	4+1	4+2	4+3	4+4	4+5	4+6	4+7	4+8	4+9	4+10
5	5+0	5+1	5+2	5+3	5+4	5+5	5+6	5+7	5+8	5+9	5+10
6	6+0	6+1	6+2	6+3	6+4	6+5	6+6	6+7	6+8	6+9	6+10
7	7+0	7+1	7+2	7+3	7+4	7+5	7+6	7+7	7+8	7+9	7+10
8	8+0	8+1	8+2	8+3	8+4	8+5	8+6	8+7	8+8	8+9	8+10
9	9+0	9+1	9+2	9+3	9+4	9+5	9+6	9+7	9+8	9+9	9+10
10	10+0	10+1	10+2	10+3	10+4	10+5	10+6	10+7	10+8	10+9	10+10

Mixed Strategies Practice

Name _____

Double Up and Color

Solve the **Doubles** and **Doubles Plus One** facts on the addition chart.
Shade the boxes with the correct color.

Doubles—blue   **Doubles Plus One**—orange

+	0	1	2	3	4	5	6	7	8	9	10
0	0+0	0+1	0+2	0+3	0+4	0+5	0+6	0+7	0+8	0+9	0+10
1	1+0	1+1	1+2	1+3	1+4	1+5	1+6	1+7	1+8	1+9	1+10
2	2+0	2+1	2+2	2+3	2+4	2+5	2+6	2+7	2+8	2+9	2+10
3	3+0	3+1	3+2	3+3	3+4	3+5	3+6	3+7	3+8	3+9	3+10
4	4+0	4+1	4+2	4+3	4+4	4+5	4+6	4+7	4+8	4+9	4+10
5	5+0	5+1	5+2	5+3	5+4	5+5	5+6	5+7	5+8	5+9	5+10
6	6+0	6+1	6+2	6+3	6+4	6+5	6+6	6+7	6+8	6+9	6+10
7	7+0	7+1	7+2	7+3	7+4	7+5	7+6	7+7	7+8	7+9	7+10
8	8+0	8+1	8+2	8+3	8+4	8+5	8+6	8+7	8+8	8+9	8+10
9	9+0	9+1	9+2	9+3	9+4	9+5	9+6	9+7	9+8	9+9	9+10
10	10+0	10+1	10+2	10+3	10+4	10+5	10+6	10+7	10+8	10+9	10+10

Mixed Strategies Practice

Name _____

It's a Mystery

Solve the **Tens Partners** and **Plus Ten** facts on the addition chart.
Shade the boxes with the correct color.

> **Tens Partners**—red   **Plus Ten**—blue

+	0	1	2	3	4	5	6	7	8	9	10
0	0+0	0+1	0+2	0+3	0+4	0+5	0+6	0+7	0+8	0+9	0+10
1	1+0	1+1	1+2	1+3	1+4	1+5	1+6	1+7	1+8	1+9	1+10
2	2+0	2+1	2+2	2+3	2+4	2+5	2+6	2+7	2+8	2+9	2+10
3	3+0	3+1	3+2	3+3	3+4	3+5	3+6	3+7	3+8	3+9	3+10
4	4+0	4+1	4+2	4+3	4+4	4+5	4+6	4+7	4+8	4+9	4+10
5	5+0	5+1	5+2	5+3	5+4	5+5	5+6	5+7	5+8	5+9	5+10
6	6+0	6+1	6+2	6+3	6+4	6+5	6+6	6+7	6+8	6+9	6+10
7	7+0	7+1	7+2	7+3	7+4	7+5	7+6	7+7	7+8	7+9	7+10
8	8+0	8+1	8+2	8+3	8+4	8+5	8+6	8+7	8+8	8+9	8+10
9	9+0	9+1	9+2	9+3	9+4	9+5	9+6	9+7	9+8	9+9	9+10
10	10+0	10+1	10+2	10+3	10+4	10+5	10+6	10+7	10+8	10+9	10+10

Mixed Strategies Practice

Name _____

Addition

Strategy Names

~~Count Up~~	Doubles Plus One	Doubles
Plus Ten	Tens Partners	Plus Zero

Complete each series. Write the strategy name.

Strategy name
Count Up

8 + 1 = 9

9 + 3 = ____

14 + 2 = ____

19 + 1 = ____

Strategy name

5 + 5 = ____

8 + 8 = ____

7 + 7 = ____

6 + 6 = ____

Strategy name

0 + 10 = ____

8 + 2 = ____

4 + 6 = ____

5 + 5 = ____

Strategy name

3 + 4 = ____

4 + 5 = ____

5 + 6 = ____

7 + 8 = ____

Strategy name

8 + 10 = ____

9 + 10 = ____

7 + 10 = ____

5 + 10 = ____

Strategy name

9 + 0 = ____

15 + 0 = ____

4 + 0 = ____

12 + 0 = ____

Mixed Strategies Practice

Name _____

Addition Power

Add and color.

9 + 9	3 + 4	8 + 2	7 + 8	10 + 8
5 + 1	9 + 2	3 + 9	13 + 3	4 + 4
1 + 9	12 + 2	8 + 8	6 + 0	6 + 3
10 + 2	14 + 3	3 + 5	3 + 6	7 + 7
16 + 3	2 + 6	3 + 7	7 + 6	16 + 2
5 + 2	4 + 6	6 + 6	18 + 1	4 + 2

If the sum is between	Color the square
0 and 8	yellow
9 and 11	red
12 and 15	green
16 and 20	blue

Building Math Fluency • EMC 3033 • © Evan-Moor Corp.

Teaching Subtraction Strategies

Pages 47–75 present practice with subtraction strategies that promote computational fluency and fact mastery.

There are two ways to look at subtraction:

- as the comparison of two quantities
  "The difference between 16 and 7 is 9."

- as the changing of an amount to less
  "If I take 7 away from 16, I have 9 left."

$$16 - 7 = 9$$

Minus Zero means subtract 0 from any number and the number stays the same.

$$3 - 0 = 3$$

A Number Minus Itself means that a number subtracted from itself is 0.

$$5 - 5 = 0 \qquad 8 - 8 = 0 \qquad 3 - 3 = 0$$

Count Back to take away small numbers, such as 1, 2, or 3.

$$4 - 1 = 3 \qquad 4 - 2 = 2 \qquad 4 - 3 = 1$$

Count Up to find the difference. This strategy is best when the numbers are close together.

$$11 - 9 = 2 \quad \text{Count up two from 9 to 11.}$$

Think Addition means that every subtraction fact is the reverse of an addition fact.

$$6 + 2 = 8 \quad \text{so} \quad 8 - 2 = 6$$

Tens Partners are helpful because if you know the addition pairs, then you know the related subtraction facts.

$$7 + 3 = 10 \qquad \text{so} \qquad 10 - 3 = 7 \qquad \text{and} \qquad 10 - 7 = 3$$

Doubles are helpful because if you know the addition Doubles facts, then you know the related subtraction facts.

$$8 + 8 = 16 \quad \text{so} \quad 16 - 8 = 8$$

Minus Ten means that when 10 is subtracted from a number, the tens-place digit decreases by one, while the ones-place digit stays the same.

$$30 - 10 = 20$$

Subtraction Strategies

Minus Zero	Subtract 0 from a number and the number stays the same. $3 - 0 = 3$
A Number Minus Itself	Subtract a number from itself and the result is 0. $3 - 3 = 0$
Count Back $-1, -2, -3$	Count Back to take away small numbers, such as 1, 2, or 3. $11 - 2 = 9$ Start at 11 and count back two.
Count Up	Count Up to find the difference when the numbers are close together. $11 - 9 = 2$ Count up two from 9 to 11.
Think Addition	Every subtraction problem can be solved as addition. $3 + 1 = 4$ so $4 - 1 = 3$
Tens Partners	If you know the Tens Partners, then you know the related subtraction facts. $9 + 1 = 10$ so $10 - 1 = 9$
Doubles	If you know the addition Doubles facts, then you know the related subtraction facts. $2 + 2 = 4$ so $4 - 2 = 2$
Minus Ten	Subtract 10 and the tens-place digit decreases by one, while the ones-place digit stays the same. $30 - 10 = 20$

Building Math Fluency • EMC 3033 • © Evan-Moor Corp.

Strategy

Minus Zero

Subtract 0 and the number stays the same.

$$3 - 0 = 3$$

Subtract 0.

$5 - 0 = \boxed{}$ $8 - 0 = \boxed{}$

$9 - 0 = \boxed{}$ $14 - 0 = \boxed{}$

$5 - \boxed{} = 5$ $12 - \boxed{} = 12$

Find the difference.

$95 - 0 = \boxed{}$ $86 - 0 = \boxed{}$

$104 - 0 = \boxed{}$ $56 - 0 = \boxed{}$

Write and solve your own **Minus Zero** problems.

$$\boxed{} \qquad \boxed{} \qquad \boxed{}$$
$$\underline{-\ 0} \qquad \underline{-\ 0} \qquad \underline{-\ 0}$$
$$\boxed{} \qquad \boxed{} \qquad \boxed{}$$

I love math.

$- 0 =$

Strategy
A Number Minus Itself

Name _____

Subtract a number from itself and the result is 0.

$$6 - 6 = 0$$

Subtract the number from itself.

$4 - 4 = \boxed{}$ $6 - 6 = \boxed{}$

$7 - 7 = \boxed{}$ $8 - 8 = \boxed{}$

$3 - \boxed{} = 0$ $12 - \boxed{} = 0$

$15 - \boxed{} = 0$ $9 - 9 = \boxed{}$

Write problems in which the difference is 0.

$\boxed{} - \boxed{} = 0$ $\boxed{} - \boxed{} = 0$

$$\begin{array}{r} \boxed{} \\ -\ \boxed{} \\ \hline 0 \end{array}$$ $$\begin{array}{r} \boxed{} \\ -\ \boxed{} \\ \hline 0 \end{array}$$ $$\begin{array}{r} \boxed{} \\ -\ \boxed{} \\ \hline 0 \end{array}$$

48 **Subtraction**

Strategy

Which Strategy Fits?

Minus Zero
Subtract 0 and the
number stays the same.

$$5 - 0 = 5$$

A Number Minus Itself
Subtract a number from
itself and the result is 0.

$$5 - 5 = 0$$

Circle the **Minus Zero** problems in blue.
Circle the **Number Minus Itself** problems in yellow.
Solve the problems.

$6 - 6 =$ _____ $4 - 0 =$ _____ $10 - 10 =$ _____

$3 - 0 =$ _____ $9 - 9 =$ _____ $17 - 0 =$ _____

$8 - 8 =$ _____ $6 - 0 =$ _____ $19 - 19 =$ _____

$3 - 3 =$ _____ $7 - 0 =$ _____ $24 - 24 =$ _____

$$\begin{array}{r} 7 \\ -7 \\ \hline \end{array} \qquad \begin{array}{r} 5 \\ -0 \\ \hline \end{array} \qquad \begin{array}{r} 13 \\ -13 \\ \hline \end{array} \qquad \begin{array}{r} 15 \\ -15 \\ \hline \end{array} \qquad \begin{array}{r} 26 \\ -0 \\ \hline \end{array} \qquad \begin{array}{r} 34 \\ -34 \\ \hline \end{array}$$

Strategy
Count Back
–1, –2, –3

Count Back to take away small numbers, such as 1, 2, or 3.

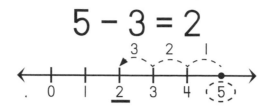

$$5 - 3 = 2$$

Use the number line to **Count Back**.

Start at 9 and count back 2.

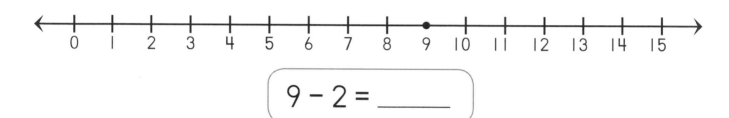

$$9 - 2 = \underline{\qquad}$$

Start at 8 and count back 3.

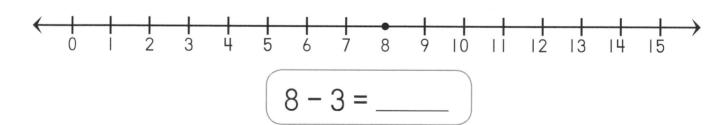

$$8 - 3 = \underline{\qquad}$$

Start at 13 and count back 2.

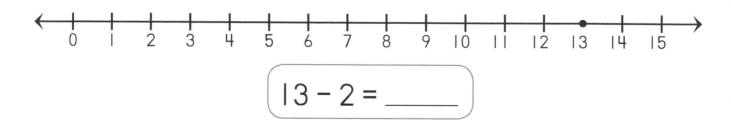

$$13 - 2 = \underline{\qquad}$$

Strategy
Count Back
-1, -2, -3

Count Back to take away small numbers, such as 1, 2, or 3.

Count Back to find the difference.
Use the number line if you like.

$$5 - 1 = \underline{\quad} \qquad 10 - 2 = \underline{\quad} \qquad 14 - 3 = \underline{\quad}$$

$$12 - 1 = \underline{\quad} \qquad 8 - 2 = \underline{\quad} \qquad 9 - 3 = \underline{\quad}$$

$$11 - 2 = \underline{\quad} \qquad 6 - 3 = \underline{\quad} \qquad 3 - 1 = \underline{\quad}$$

$$9 - 2 = \underline{\quad} \qquad 14 - 1 = \underline{\quad} \qquad 5 - 3 = \underline{\quad}$$

$$12 - 3 = \underline{\quad} \qquad 7 - 1 = \underline{\quad} \qquad 13 - 2 = \underline{\quad}$$

8	15	4	10	6	6
− 3	− 1	− 3	− 1	− 1	− 2

Strategy
Count Back
-1, -2, -3

Count Back to take away small numbers, such as 1, 2, or 3.

Start at the first number.
Count Back in your head. Write the difference.

5 − 2 = ___3___

9 − 2 = ___7___

8 − 3 = ___5___

8 − 2 = _____

6 − 2 = _____

5 − 1 = _____

9 − 3 = _____

8 − 1 = _____

7 − 3 = _____

9 − 1 = _____

7 − 2 = _____

6 − 3 = _____

10 − 3 = _____

11 − 2 = _____

12 − 3 = _____

Building Math Fluency • EMC 3033 • © Evan-Moor Corp.

Strategy
Count Back
−1, −2, −3

Count Back to take away small
numbers, such as 1, 2, or 3.

Count Back to subtract.
Use the number line if you like.

$6 - 2 = \boxed{}$ $8 - 3 = \boxed{}$

$12 - 1 = \boxed{}$ $7 - 2 = \boxed{}$

$9 - 3 = \boxed{}$ $14 - 1 = \boxed{}$

Complete the equations.

$12 - \boxed{} = 11$ $7 - \boxed{} = 6$

$8 - \boxed{} = 6$ $15 - \boxed{} = 12$

$6 - \boxed{} = 3$ $18 - \boxed{} = 16$

Write your own equations.

$\boxed{} - 2 = \boxed{}$ $\boxed{} - 3 = \boxed{}$

$\boxed{} - 1 = \boxed{}$ $\boxed{} - 2 = \boxed{}$

```
22
21
20
19
18
17
16
15
14
13
12
11
10
9
8
7
6
5
4
3
2
1
0
```

Count Up

Name _____

Count Up to find the difference between numbers.

Start at 9. **Count Up** to 11.
The number of hops is the difference.

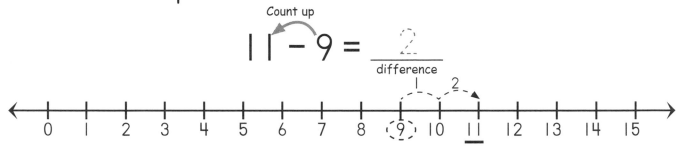

Count up

$$11 - 9 = \underline{2}$$

difference

Start at 11. **Count Up** to 14.
The number of hops is the difference.

$$14 - 11 = \underline{\hphantom{000}}$$

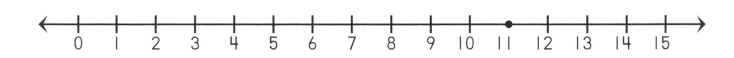

Start at 9. **Count Up** to 13.
The number of hops is the difference.

$$13 - 9 = \underline{\hphantom{000}}$$

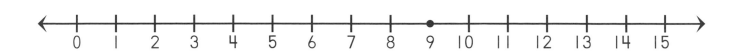

Building Math Fluency • EMC 3033 • © Evan-Moor Corp.

Count Up

Count Up to find the difference between numbers.

Count Up from the bottom number with tally marks. Solve.

$$8 - 5 = 3$$ |||

$$7 - 5 =$$

$$9 - 6 =$$

$$6 - 4 =$$

$$11 - 9 =$$

$$12 - 9 =$$

$$7 - 6 =$$

$$9 - 7 =$$

$$16 - 13 =$$

$$15 - 12 =$$

$$8 - 7 =$$

$$14 - 13 =$$

$$12 - 11 =$$

$$17 - 15 =$$

$$16 - 14 =$$

$$18 - 17 =$$

Count Up

Name _____

Count Up to find the difference between numbers.

Make dots to **Count Up** from the smaller number.
Count the dots to find the difference.

14,15 15 − 13 = __2__	9,10,11 11 − 8 = __3__	9 − 7 = _____
14 − 12 = _____	12 − 9 = _____	8 − 6 = _____
11 − 9 = _____	10 − 8 = _____	7 − 5 = _____
15 − 12 = _____	13 − 11 = _____	14 − 13 = _____
10 − 9 = _____	12 − 10 = _____	16 − 14 = _____
13 − 10 = _____	16 − 13 = _____	12 − 11 = _____

Strategy

Count Up

Count Up to find the difference between numbers.

Count Up to subtract.
Start at the second number and count up to the first number.

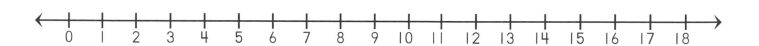

$5 - 4 =$ _____ $9 - 8 =$ _____

$7 - 5 =$ _____ $7 - 4 =$ _____

$8 - 6 =$ _____ $9 - 7 =$ _____

$6 - 4 =$ _____ $8 - 5 =$ _____

$10 - 8 =$ _____ $14 - 12 =$ _____

$15 - 13 =$ _____ $18 - 15 =$ _____

Strategy

Which Strategy Fits?

Count Back

Count back when subtracting a small number. **Count Back** works for −1, −2, and −3 problems.

$$100 - 2 = \underline{98}$$

It is fast to count back 2.

Count Up

Count up when subtracting a large number. **Count Up** works best when the numbers in the problem are close together.

$$100 - 99 = \underline{1}$$

It is too far to count back 99. It is easy to count up from 99.

Circle **Count Back** problems in blue.
Circle **Count Up** problems in red.
Solve.

$$20 - 17 = \underline{\hspace{2cm}}$$

$$17 - 15 = \underline{\hspace{2cm}}$$

$$14 - 2 = \underline{\hspace{2cm}}$$

$$14 - 3 = \underline{\hspace{2cm}}$$

$$9 - 7 = \underline{\hspace{2cm}}$$

$$16 - 14 = \underline{\hspace{2cm}}$$

$$15 - 3 = \underline{\hspace{2cm}}$$

$$19 - 1 = \underline{\hspace{2cm}}$$

   Building Math Fluency • EMC 3033 • © Evan-Moor Corp.

Strategy

Think Addition

Name _____

$$7 - 5 = \boxed{2} \text{ is the same as } 2 + \boxed{5} = 7$$

add

Solve the subtraction problems. Rewrite them as addition problems.

Subtraction		Addition
$9 - 2 = \square$ (add)	↻→	$7 + \square = 9$
$10 - 7 = \square$	↻→	$3 + \square = 10$
$7 - 4 = \square$	↻→	$\square + \square = 7$
$8 - 6 = \square$	↻→	$\square + \square = 8$
$6 - 3 = \square$	↻→	$\square + \square = 6$
$10 - 6 = \square$	↻→	$4 + \square = 10$
$9 - 5 = \square$	↻→	$4 + \square = 9$

Strategy
Think Addition

Every subtraction problem can be solved as addition.

Solve the problems. Match the addition facts to the related subtraction facts.

Add	Match	Subtract
4 + 4 = __8__		11 – 5 = _____
6 + 5 = _____		8 – 4 = __4__
7 + 7 = _____		14 – 7 = _____
8 + 7 = _____		12 – 9 = _____
3 + 9 = _____		13 – 2 = _____
11 + 2 = _____		15 – 7 = _____
12 + 3 = _____		15 – 3 = _____

Write two addition facts. Match them to the related subtraction facts.

Add	Match	Subtract
_____		_____
_____		_____

 Building Math Fluency • EMC 3033 • © Evan-Moor Corp.

Strategy
Tens Partners

If you know the **Tens Partners**, then you know the related subtraction facts.

Color the dots to show the number given.
Count the rest of the dots. Write the number.

$4 + \underline{} = 10$

$\underline{} + 7 = 10$

$\underline{} + 8 = 10$

$5 + \underline{} = 10$

$0 + \underline{} = 10$

$\underline{} + 9 = 10$

Use the **Tens Partners** facts to complete the equations.

$10 - \underline{} = \underline{}$

$10 - \underline{} = \underline{}$

$10 - \underline{} = \underline{}$

$10 - \underline{} = \underline{}$

Tens Partners

Name _____

If you know the **Tens Partners**, then you know the related subtraction facts.

Match the addition facts to the subtraction facts.
Write the answers.

Tens Partners Addition		Tens Partners Subtraction	

8 2	10 10
+ 2 + 8	− 3 − 7
10 10	

3 7	10 10
+ 7 + 3	− 8 − 2
	2 8

| 1   9 | 10   10 |
| + 9   + 1 | − 5   − 5 |

| 6   4 | 10   10 |
| + 4   + 6 | − 6   − 4 |

| 5   5 | 10   10 |
| + 5   + 5 | − 9   − 1 |

Building Math Fluency • EMC 3033 • © Evan-Moor Corp.

Strategy

Doubles

If you know the addition **Doubles**, then you know the related subtraction facts.

Draw dots to show **Doubles**. Add.

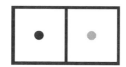

$1 + \underline{} = 2$

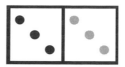

$3 + \underline{} = 6$

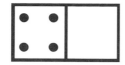

$4 + \underline{} = \underline{}$

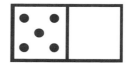

$5 + \underline{} = \underline{}$

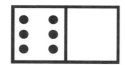

$6 + \underline{} = \underline{}$

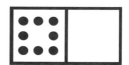

$8 + \underline{} = \underline{}$

Count the dots. Cross out one double. Subtract.

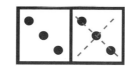

$6 - 3 = 3$

$\underline{} - \underline{} = \underline{}$

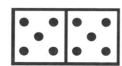

$\underline{} - \underline{} = \underline{}$

$\underline{} - \underline{} = \underline{}$

Strategy

Doubles

If you know the addition **Doubles** facts, then you know the related subtraction facts.

Do the addition facts first. Then use addition to solve the subtraction facts.

Doubles Addition		Doubles Subtraction	
5 + 5	7 + 7	10 − 5	14 − 7
8 + 8	3 + 3	16 − 8	6 − 3
4 + 4	6 + 6	8 − 4	12 − 6
9 + 9	2 + 2	18 − 9	4 − 2
10 +10	11 +11	20 −10	22 −11

Building Math Fluency • EMC 3033 • © Evan-Moor Corp.

Strategy

Minus Ten

When you subtract 10, the tens-place digit decreases by one, and the ones-place digit stays the same.

Use the number grid to help you jump back 10 each time.

1	2	3	4	5	6	7	8	9	10
11	12	13	14	15	16	17	18	19	20
21	22	23	24	25	26	27	28	29	30

30 – 10 = _____   22 – 10 = _____

20 – 10 = _____   28 – 10 = _____

29 – 10 = _____   24 – 10 = _____

17 – 10 = _____   18 – 10 = _____

15 – 10 = _____   13 – 10 = _____

25 – 10 = _____   19 – 10 = _____

Strategy

Minus Ten

When you subtract 10,
the tens-place digit decreases
by one, and the ones-place digit
stays the same.

Use the number grid to help you jump back 10 each time.

1	2	3	4	5	6	7	8	9	10
11	12	13	14	15	16	17	18	19	20
21	22	23	24	25	26	27	28	29	30
31	32	33	34	35	36	37	38	39	40
41	42	43	44	45	46	47	48	49	50
51	52	53	54	55	56	57	58	59	60

50 – 10 = _____   28 – 10 = _____

40 – 10 = _____   33 – 10 = _____

39 – 10 = _____   24 – 10 = _____

30 – 10 = _____   15 – 10 = _____

57 – 10 = _____   46 – 10 = _____

     Building Math Fluency • EMC 3033 • © Evan-Moor Corp.

Strategy

Minus Ten

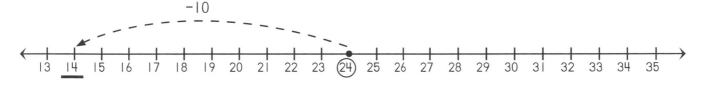

When you subtract 10,
the tens-place digit decreases
by one, and the ones-place digit
stays the same.

Show 24 − 10 = **14**

−10

13 14 15 16 17 18 19 20 21 22 23 (24) 25 26 27 28 29 30 31 32 33 34 35

Jump back 10 on the number line.

Show 32 − 10 = _____

13 14 15 16 17 18 19 20 21 22 23 24 25 26 27 28 29 30 31 32 33 34 35

Show 51 − 10 = _____

40 41 42 43 44 45 46 47 48 49 50 51 52 53 54 55 56 57 58 59 60 61 62

Show 64 − 10 = _____

50 51 52 53 54 55 56 57 58 59 60 61 62 63 64 65 66 67 68 69 70 71 72

Mixed
Strategies
Practice

Name _____

Subtraction Strategies

> ~~Count Up~~   Doubles   A Number Minus Itself
>
> Minus Zero   Minus Ten   Tens Partners

Complete each series. Write the strategy name.

Strategy name

Count Up

$20 - 18 = \underline{\ 2\ }$

$14 - 13 = \underline{\qquad}$

$19 - 17 = \underline{\qquad}$

$11 - 9 = \underline{\qquad}$

$12 - 8 = \underline{\qquad}$

Strategy name

$10 - 4 = \underline{\qquad}$

$10 - 8 = \underline{\qquad}$

$10 - 7 = \underline{\qquad}$

$10 - 5 = \underline{\qquad}$

$10 - 3 = \underline{\qquad}$

Strategy name

$9 - 9 = \underline{\qquad}$

$8 - 8 = \underline{\qquad}$

$4 - 4 = \underline{\qquad}$

$5 - 5 = \underline{\qquad}$

$7 - 7 = \underline{\qquad}$

Strategy name

$10 - 5 = \underline{\qquad}$

$12 - 6 = \underline{\qquad}$

$6 - 3 = \underline{\qquad}$

$14 - 7 = \underline{\qquad}$

$20 - 10 = \underline{\qquad}$

Strategy name

$18 - 10 = \underline{\qquad}$

$19 - 10 = \underline{\qquad}$

$17 - 10 = \underline{\qquad}$

$15 - 10 = \underline{\qquad}$

$16 - 10 = \underline{\qquad}$

Strategy name

$18 - 0 = \underline{\qquad}$

$16 - 0 = \underline{\qquad}$

$14 - 0 = \underline{\qquad}$

$12 - 0 = \underline{\qquad}$

$8 - 0 = \underline{\qquad}$

Building Math Fluency • EMC 3033 • © Evan-Moor Corp.

Mixed Strategies Practice

Which Strategy Fits?

Write each fact under the best strategy.
Solve the problems.

Count Back $-1, -2, -3$

Doubles

Tens Partners
$10 - 7 = 3$

Minus Ten

Cross out the facts you use.

~~10 – 7~~	10 – 2	12 – 6
16 – 1	18 – 2	50 – 10
40 – 10	18 – 9	8 – 4
10 – 4	13 – 2	30 – 10

Subtraction 69

Mixed Strategies Practice

Subtraction Challenge

Name _____

Subtract and color.

16 − 8	9 − 3	12 − 4	10 − 4	9 − 3
7 − 0	15 − 3	6 − 6	18 − 3	8 − 1
18 − 9	12 − 12	11 − 2	4 − 0	20 − 10
10 − 5	14 − 3	11 − 8	10 − 1	7 − 2
8 − 3	12 − 3	19 − 10	11 − 2	12 − 7
20 − 0	18 − 2	17 − 1	19 − 3	16 − 0

If the difference is between	Color the square
0 and 5	white
6 and 8	yellow
9 and 11	red
12 and 15	blue
16 and 20	green

Building Math Fluency • EMC 3033 • © Evan-Moor Corp.

Mixed Strategies Practice

Name _____

Match the Facts

Use addition to solve subtraction.
Solve and match.

Tens Partners Addition and Subtraction

4 + 6 = __10__   10 – 5 = _____

2 + 8 = _____   10 – 6 = __4__

3 + 7 = _____   10 – 8 = _____

1 + 9 = _____   10 – 9 = _____

5 + 5 = _____   10 – 7 = _____

Doubles Addition and Subtraction

5 + 5 = _____   12 – 6 = _____

6 + 6 = _____   14 – 7 = _____

7 + 7 = _____   16 – 8 = _____

8 + 8 = _____   10 – 5 = _____

9 + 9 = _____   18 – 9 = _____

Name _____

Match the Facts

Solve the problems. Cut and glue each fact under the best strategy.

Count Back −1, −2, −3

Doubles

Tens Partners

Minus Ten

---

30 − 10 =	11 − 2 =	10 − 5 =
10 − 6 =	12 − 2 =	40 − 10 =
9 − 3 =	8 − 4 =	10 − 7 =

Name _____

Match the Strategies

Solve the problems. Cut and glue each fact under the best strategy.

A Number Minus Itself

Minus Ten

Doubles

Count Up

50 − 10 =	18 − 16 =	4 − 2 =
10 − 8 =	9 − 9 =	60 − 10 =
15 − 15 =	12 − 6 =	

Mixed Strategies Practice

Hungry Bunnies

Help the bunnies find lunch.
Solve the problems. Color the paths.

Minus Zero
Color it **yellow**.

Tens Partners
Color it **green**.

Minus Ten
Color it **orange**.

8 − 0	9 − 8	10 − 3	10 − 6	30 −10
6 − 0	5 − 0	12 − 9	10 − 9	70 −10
16 − 6	7 − 0	10 − 5	10 − 7	40 −10
3 − 0	12 − 0	10 − 2	18 −10	24 −10
19 − 0	9 − 3	10 − 4	35 −10	80 −10

Minus Zero

Tens Partners

Minus Ten

Building Math Fluency • EMC 3033 • © Evan-Moor Corp.

Mixed Strategies Practice

Name _____

Lost Bunnies

Help the Mother Bunnies find their babies.
Match the strategies to the facts.

Count Back •

Count Up •

Tens Partners •

Doubles •

Minus Ten •

$7 - 2 =$ _____

$8 - 1 =$ _____

$12 - 6 =$ _____

$18 - 9 =$ _____

$10 - 5 =$ _____

$10 - 3 =$ _____

$15 - 13 =$ _____

$20 - 18 =$ _____

$30 - 10 =$ _____

$50 - 10 =$ _____

How to Use
Test Your Skills

The *Test Your Skills* exercises on pages 79–107 provide multiple opportunities for assessment of computational skills. Each test series—for addition and subtraction—begins with easier problems and increases in difficulty.

Each page in the *Test Your Skills* section can be used multiple times and in different ways to build computational skills and improve fact fluency.

Mixed Strategies Practice

The tests provide the opportunity to practice many of the computational strategies presented in the first part of this book. For each problem, students should ask themselves: Which strategy best suits the numbers involved?

Strategy Focus

Have students select one strategy at a time to practice. They examine the problems and then circle and solve those that fit the focus strategy.

Assessment

Use the tests to determine how students are progressing in their acquisition of computational skills. If appropriate, allow students to set their own goals for improvement of computation speed.

Student Self-Evaluation

The record area at the bottom of each *Test Your Skills* page affords students the opportunity to assess their own performance and use of computational strategies. This self-evaluation is an important part of the skill-building process.

Student Assessment/Record

Name

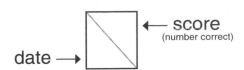

date → score (number correct)

Test Levels	Addition—Sums						Subtraction—Minuends					
0 to 7												
7 to 10												
10 to 12												
13 to 15												
15 to 17												
15 to 20												
18 to 20												

Notes:

Class Assessment/Record

Students	Addition—Sums					Subtraction—Minuends					
	0 to 7	7 to 10	10 to 12	13 to 15	15 to 20	0 to 7	7 to 10	10 to 12	13 to 15	15 to 17	18 to 20

Building Math Fluency • EMC 3033 • © Evan-Moor Corp.

Name _____   My Score _____

Test Your Skills

$$\begin{array}{r} 0 \\ + 0 \\ \hline \end{array}$$ $$\begin{array}{r} 1 \\ + 1 \\ \hline \end{array}$$ $$\begin{array}{r} 2 \\ + 1 \\ \hline \end{array}$$ $$\begin{array}{r} 3 \\ + 0 \\ \hline \end{array}$$ $$\begin{array}{r} 3 \\ + 2 \\ \hline \end{array}$$ $$\begin{array}{r} 4 \\ + 0 \\ \hline \end{array}$$

$$\begin{array}{r} 4 \\ + 2 \\ \hline \end{array}$$ $$\begin{array}{r} 4 \\ + 3 \\ \hline \end{array}$$ $$\begin{array}{r} 5 \\ + 1 \\ \hline \end{array}$$ $$\begin{array}{r} 5 \\ + 2 \\ \hline \end{array}$$ $$\begin{array}{r} 1 \\ + 5 \\ \hline \end{array}$$ $$\begin{array}{r} 6 \\ + 1 \\ \hline \end{array}$$

$$\begin{array}{r} 2 \\ + 3 \\ \hline \end{array}$$ $$\begin{array}{r} 2 \\ + 2 \\ \hline \end{array}$$ $$\begin{array}{r} 7 \\ + 0 \\ \hline \end{array}$$ $$\begin{array}{r} 3 \\ + 2 \\ \hline \end{array}$$ $$\begin{array}{r} 2 \\ + 4 \\ \hline \end{array}$$ $$\begin{array}{r} 3 \\ + 3 \\ \hline \end{array}$$

$$\begin{array}{r} 1 \\ + 0 \\ \hline \end{array}$$ $$\begin{array}{r} 2 \\ + 0 \\ \hline \end{array}$$ $$\begin{array}{r} 1 \\ + 1 \\ \hline \end{array}$$ $$\begin{array}{r} 3 \\ + 1 \\ \hline \end{array}$$ $$\begin{array}{r} 3 \\ + 3 \\ \hline \end{array}$$ $$\begin{array}{r} 4 \\ + 1 \\ \hline \end{array}$$

$$\begin{array}{r} 4 \\ + 3 \\ \hline \end{array}$$ $$\begin{array}{r} 5 \\ + 0 \\ \hline \end{array}$$ $$\begin{array}{r} 5 \\ + 2 \\ \hline \end{array}$$ $$\begin{array}{r} 1 \\ + 2 \\ \hline \end{array}$$ $$\begin{array}{r} 6 \\ + 0 \\ \hline \end{array}$$ $$\begin{array}{r} 1 \\ + 6 \\ \hline \end{array}$$

$$\begin{array}{r} 1 \\ + 3 \\ \hline \end{array}$$ $$\begin{array}{r} 4 \\ + 2 \\ \hline \end{array}$$ $$\begin{array}{r} 1 \\ + 4 \\ \hline \end{array}$$ $$\begin{array}{r} 4 \\ + 3 \\ \hline \end{array}$$ $$\begin{array}{r} 2 \\ + 5 \\ \hline \end{array}$$ $$\begin{array}{r} 0 \\ + 7 \\ \hline \end{array}$$

How am I doing?

Accuracy
❏ I got them all right!
❏ I missed a couple.
❏ I will practice these:
  (List up to 3 facts.)

Efficiency
I used these strategies:
❏ Plus Zero
❏ Count Up +1, +2, +3
❏ Doubles/Doubles Plus One

Time
I finished in:
_____

My next goal is:
_____

Name _____   My Score _____

Test Your Skills

4 + 0	4 + 3	4 + 1	4 + 2	3 + 2	3 + 1
2 + 2	2 + 1	1 + 1	1 + 0	7 + 0	1 + 6
2 + 4	1 + 3	6 + 1	2 + 4	1 + 5	2 + 2
5 + 2	2 + 3	2 + 5	3 + 4	5 + 2	4 + 1
4 + 2	3 + 3	5 + 0	3 + 0	2 + 4	0 + 0
2 + 5	5 + 1	6 + 1	4 + 3	6 + 0	2 + 3

How am I doing?

Accuracy
❏ I got them all right!
❏ I missed a couple.
❏ I will practice these:
(List up to 3 facts.)

Efficiency
I used these strategies:
❏ Plus Zero
❏ Count Up +1, +2, +3
❏ Doubles/Doubles Plus One

Time
I finished in:

_____

My next goal is:

_____

Name _____   My Score _____

Test Your Skills

10 + 0	8 + 2	5 + 4	4 + 6	2 + 6	6 + 2
9 + 1	7 + 3	5 + 5	2 + 7	1 + 9	8 + 1
8 + 2	4 + 5	6 + 3	6 + 4	7 + 2	5 + 3
8 + 1	5 + 3	2 + 5	1 + 7	2 + 8	9 + 0
1 + 9	4 + 4	3 + 6	0 + 8	4 + 6	3 + 4
3 + 7	4 + 6	3 + 5	2 + 7	5 + 4	9 + 0

How am I doing?

Accuracy
❏ I got them all right!
❏ I missed a couple.
❏ I will practice these:
(List up to 3 facts.)

Efficiency
I used these strategies:
❏ Plus Zero
❏ Count Up +1, +2, +3
❏ Doubles/Doubles Plus One
❏ Tens Partners

Time
I finished in:
_____

My next goal is:
_____

Name _____   My Score _____

Test Your Skills

5 + 4	1 + 9	3 + 5	10 + 0	6 + 3	9 + 0
8 + 2	4 + 5	3 + 7	6 + 4	5 + 5	3 + 4
8 + 0	7 + 2	4 + 4	6 + 1	2 + 8	5 + 3
4 + 3	2 + 5	3 + 6	9 + 1	8 + 0	8 + 2
3 + 4	2 + 6	5 + 5	7 + 0	4 + 3	7 + 2
8 + 1	3 + 6	5 + 2	1 + 7	6 + 2	7 + 3

How am I doing?

Accuracy
- ❏ I got them all right!
- ❏ I missed a couple.
- ❏ I will practice these:
  (List up to 3 facts.)

Efficiency
I used these strategies:
- ❏ Plus Zero
- ❏ Count Up +1, +2, +3
- ❏ Doubles/Doubles Plus One
- ❏ Tens Partners

Time
I finished in:

_____

My next goal is:

_____

Name _____   My Score _____

Test Your Skills

8 + 2	3 + 4	5 + 5	3 + 6	2 + 7	1 + 8
9 + 0	7 + 2	5 + 3	9 + 1	4 + 5	3 + 3
2 + 7	1 + 9	8 + 0	8 + 2	4 + 3	5 + 5
2 + 6	8 + 1	6 + 3	7 + 3	2 + 5	4 + 4
7 + 3	4 + 5	6 + 4	4 + 2	6 + 2	5 + 1
5 + 2	4 + 6	5 + 4	3 + 2	3 + 7	2 + 8

How am I doing?

Accuracy
❑ I got them all right!
❑ I missed a couple.
❑ I will practice these:
(List up to 3 facts.)

Efficiency
I used these strategies:
❑ Plus Zero
❑ Count Up +1, +2, +3
❑ Doubles/Doubles Plus One
❑ Tens Partners

Time
I finished in:

_____

My next goal is:

_____

Name _____   My Score _____

Test Your Skills

10 + 0	10 + 2	6 + 4	9 + 2	3 + 8	6 + 6
11 + 1	7 + 3	5 + 5	4 + 8	9 + 1	12 + 0
8 + 3	7 + 5	3 + 7	10 + 2	5 + 7	8 + 4
10 + 1	9 + 3	6 + 5	4 + 7	2 + 9	11 + 0
7 + 4	10 + 1	8 + 4	2 + 8	12 + 0	3 + 9
4 + 6	6 + 6	7 + 5	11 + 1	5 + 6	7 + 3

How am I doing?

Accuracy
❏ I got them all right!
❏ I missed a couple.
❏ I will practice these:
(List up to 3 facts.)

Efficiency
I used these strategies:
❏ Count Up +1, +2, +3
❏ Doubles/Doubles Plus One
❏ Tens Partners
❏ Plus Ten

Time
I finished in:

_____

My next goal is:

_____

Name _____   My Score _____

Test Your Skills

11 + 1	3 + 8	10 + 2	11 + 0	4 + 6	12 + 0
5 + 5	3 + 7	7 + 5	8 + 3	5 + 7	5 + 6
2 + 8	4 + 7	9 + 1	7 + 4	6 + 5	3 + 9
12 + 0	4 + 6	8 + 4	6 + 4	5 + 5	8 + 2
10 + 2	6 + 6	10 + 1	11 + 0	10 + 2	4 + 8
7 + 3	4 + 7	8 + 3	6 + 5	7 + 5	9 + 3

How am I doing?

Accuracy
❏ I got them all right!
❏ I missed a couple.
❏ I will practice these:
   (List up to 3 facts.)

Efficiency
I used these strategies:
❏ Count Up +1, +2, +3
❏ Doubles/Doubles Plus One
❏ Tens Partners
❏ Plus Ten

Time
I finished in:
_____

My next goal is:
_____

Name _____   My Score _____

Test Your Skills

13	8	9	10	6	14
+ 0	+ 5	+ 4	+ 5	+ 7	+ 1

13	12	9	15	11	10
+ 1	+ 3	+ 5	+ 0	+ 2	+ 4

8	4	11	12	11	12
+ 6	+ 9	+ 3	+ 2	+ 4	+ 1

10	12	8	15	13	13
+ 4	+ 3	+ 7	+ 0	+ 1	+ 2

10	12	11	12	10	8
+ 3	+ 2	+ 2	+ 1	+ 5	+ 6

9	7	5	7	4	7
+ 6	+ 8	+ 8	+ 7	+ 9	+ 6

How am I doing?

Accuracy
❏ I got them all right!
❏ I missed a couple.
❏ I will practice these:
(List up to 3 facts.)

Efficiency
I used these strategies:
❏ Count Up +1, +2, +3
❏ Doubles/Doubles Plus One
❏ Tens Partners
❏ Plus Ten

Time
I finished in:
_____
My next goal is:
_____

Name _____   My Score _____

Test Your Skills

8 + 7	6 + 7	5 + 9	10 + 5	13 + 2	7 + 8
8 + 5	14 + 1	15 + 0	6 + 8	9 + 4	11 + 3
7 + 6	10 + 5	9 + 5	13 + 1	8 + 5	7 + 7
9 + 6	13 + 1	12 + 3	11 + 2	8 + 6	10 + 4
11 + 4	15 + 0	12 + 2	5 + 8	12 + 1	12 + 3
9 + 4	7 + 6	11 + 4	10 + 3	6 + 9	13 + 2

How am I doing?

Accuracy
❏ I got them all right!
❏ I missed a couple.
❏ I will practice these:
   (List up to 3 facts.)

Efficiency
I used these strategies:
❏ Count Up +1, +2, +3
❏ Doubles/Doubles Plus One
❏ Tens Partners
❏ Plus Ten

Time
I finished in:
_____

My next goal is:
_____

Name _____   My Score _____

Test Your Skills

$$\begin{array}{r} 13 \\ + 0 \\ \hline \end{array}$$
$$\begin{array}{r} 9 \\ + 5 \\ \hline \end{array}$$
$$\begin{array}{r} 8 \\ + 2 \\ \hline \end{array}$$
$$\begin{array}{r} 7 \\ + 4 \\ \hline \end{array}$$
$$\begin{array}{r} 8 \\ + 5 \\ \hline \end{array}$$
$$\begin{array}{r} 6 \\ + 6 \\ \hline \end{array}$$

$$\begin{array}{r} 11 \\ + 0 \\ \hline \end{array}$$
$$\begin{array}{r} 13 \\ + 1 \\ \hline \end{array}$$
$$\begin{array}{r} 9 \\ + 3 \\ \hline \end{array}$$
$$\begin{array}{r} 5 \\ + 4 \\ \hline \end{array}$$
$$\begin{array}{r} 6 \\ + 5 \\ \hline \end{array}$$
$$\begin{array}{r} 8 \\ + 6 \\ \hline \end{array}$$

$$\begin{array}{r} 7 \\ + 7 \\ \hline \end{array}$$
$$\begin{array}{r} 12 \\ + 2 \\ \hline \end{array}$$
$$\begin{array}{r} 9 \\ + 4 \\ \hline \end{array}$$
$$\begin{array}{r} 6 \\ + 4 \\ \hline \end{array}$$
$$\begin{array}{r} 8 \\ + 7 \\ \hline \end{array}$$
$$\begin{array}{r} 5 \\ + 7 \\ \hline \end{array}$$

$$\begin{array}{r} 8 \\ + 4 \\ \hline \end{array}$$
$$\begin{array}{r} 3 \\ + 9 \\ \hline \end{array}$$
$$\begin{array}{r} 12 \\ + 3 \\ \hline \end{array}$$
$$\begin{array}{r} 7 \\ + 3 \\ \hline \end{array}$$
$$\begin{array}{r} 14 \\ + 1 \\ \hline \end{array}$$
$$\begin{array}{r} 10 \\ + 3 \\ \hline \end{array}$$

$$\begin{array}{r} 6 \\ + 5 \\ \hline \end{array}$$
$$\begin{array}{r} 4 \\ + 5 \\ \hline \end{array}$$
$$\begin{array}{r} 5 \\ + 8 \\ \hline \end{array}$$
$$\begin{array}{r} 7 \\ + 6 \\ \hline \end{array}$$
$$\begin{array}{r} 5 \\ + 6 \\ \hline \end{array}$$
$$\begin{array}{r} 6 \\ + 9 \\ \hline \end{array}$$

$$\begin{array}{r} 8 \\ + 3 \\ \hline \end{array}$$
$$\begin{array}{r} 4 \\ + 6 \\ \hline \end{array}$$
$$\begin{array}{r} 10 \\ + 5 \\ \hline \end{array}$$
$$\begin{array}{r} 9 \\ + 2 \\ \hline \end{array}$$
$$\begin{array}{r} 5 \\ + 5 \\ \hline \end{array}$$
$$\begin{array}{r} 6 \\ + 8 \\ \hline \end{array}$$

How am I doing?

Accuracy
❏ I got them all right!
❏ I missed a couple.
❏ I will practice these:
   (List up to 3 facts.)

Efficiency
I used these strategies:
❏ Count Up +1, +2, +3
❏ Doubles/Doubles Plus One
❏ Tens Partners
❏ Plus Ten

Time
I finished in:
_____

My next goal is:
_____

Name _____   My Score _____

Test Your Skills

15 + 0	15 + 2	15 + 4	16 + 0	16 + 2	11 + 4
17 + 1	17 + 3	18 + 1	19 + 0	20 + 0	16 + 1
16 + 3	17 + 0	13 + 2	15 + 4	17 + 2	20 + 0
15 + 1	15 + 3	15 + 5	16 + 1	16 + 3	17 + 0
17 + 2	18 + 0	18 + 2	19 + 1	16 + 0	16 + 2
16 + 4	17 + 1	17 + 3	16 + 3	15 + 1	18 + 2

How am I doing?

Accuracy
- ❏ I got them all right!
- ❏ I missed a couple.
- ❏ I will practice these:
  (List up to 3 facts.)

Efficiency
I used these strategies:
- ❏ Count Up +1, +2, +3
- ❏ Doubles/Doubles Plus One
- ❏ Tens Partners
- ❏ Plus Ten

Time
I finished in:

_____

My next goal is:

_____

Name _____   My Score _____

Test Your Skills

17 + 0	17 + 2	20 + 0	12 + 3	15 + 4	17 + 2
10 + 6	19 + 1	18 + 2	16 + 4	15 + 3	17 + 3
15 + 5	20 + 0	16 + 1	17 + 1	19 + 0	18 + 1
15 + 2	14 + 2	16 + 4	15 + 0	13 + 3	15 + 4
15 + 3	16 + 3	17 + 0	15 + 1	16 + 1	15 + 5
18 + 0	16 + 0	16 + 2	17 + 2	19 + 1	18 + 2

How am I doing?

Accuracy
❑ I got them all right!
❑ I missed a couple.
❑ I will practice these:
  (List up to 3 facts.)

Efficiency
I used these strategies:
❑ Count Up +1, +2, +3
❑ Doubles/Doubles Plus One
❑ Tens Partners
❑ Plus Ten

Time
I finished in:

_____

My next goal is:

_____

Name _____   My Score _____

Test Your Skills

12 + 2	8 + 8	17 + 1	15 + 3	18 + 1	12 + 7
8 + 5	16 + 1	6 + 4	16 + 3	16 + 4	17 + 0
9 + 8	17 + 2	14 + 3	9 + 9	14 + 4	18 + 2
7 + 7	19 + 0	18 + 2	11 + 2	14 + 5	7 + 3
12 + 8	16 + 4	13 + 4	15 + 0	12 + 7	10 + 8
10 + 6	6 + 3	9 + 6	5 + 4	8 + 2	9 + 3

How am I doing?

Accuracy
- ❏ I got them all right!
- ❏ I missed a couple.
- ❏ I will practice these:
  (List up to 3 facts.)

Efficiency
I used these strategies:
- ❏ Count Up +1, +2, +3
- ❏ Doubles/Doubles Plus One
- ❏ Tens Partners
- ❏ Plus Ten

Time
I finished in:

_____

My next goal is:

_____

Name _____ My Score _____

Test Your Skills

18 + 0	7 + 7	17 + 1	9 + 4	17 + 3	12 + 6
14 + 2	10 + 7	19 + 0	8 + 8	20 + 0	14 + 4
15 + 3	19 + 1	15 + 0	6 + 5	17 + 2	11 + 4
12 + 2	9 + 5	13 + 0	17 + 0	16 + 4	12 + 7
5 + 5	6 + 3	10 + 6	7 + 6	9 + 3	8 + 9
16 + 3	12 + 1	16 + 0	9 + 9	16 + 2	9 + 7

How am I doing?

Accuracy
❏ I got them all right!
❏ I missed a couple.
❏ I will practice these:
(List up to 3 facts.)

Efficiency
I used these strategies:
❏ Count Up +1, +2, +3
❏ Doubles/Doubles Plus One
❏ Tens Partners
❏ Plus Ten

Time
I finished in:
_____
My next goal is:
_____

Name _____   My Score _____

Test Your Skills

1 - 0	3 - 1	4 - 2	5 - 0	7 - 3	6 - 5
6 - 3	7 - 5	5 - 3	7 - 1	3 - 0	1 - 1
3 - 3	4 - 1	5 - 1	6 - 1	7 - 0	6 - 6
2 - 1	3 - 2	7 - 7	5 - 5	4 - 3	7 - 2
6 - 4	7 - 2	4 - 4	7 - 6	5 - 2	2 - 0
4 - 0	7 - 4	6 - 0	6 - 6	5 - 4	6 - 2

How am I doing?

Accuracy
❏ I got them all right!
❏ I missed a couple.
❏ I will practice these:
(List up to 3 facts.)

Efficiency
I used these strategies:
❏ Minus Zero and
   A Number Minus Itself
❏ Count Back −1, −2, −3
❏ Count Up from bottom number
❏ Doubles Subtraction

Time
I finished in:
_____
My next goal is:
_____

Test Your Skills

4 − 1	7 − 5	3 − 3	5 − 1	6 − 1	7 − 6
7 − 2	2 − 2	6 − 4	7 − 4	6 − 6	2 − 0
3 − 2	5 − 4	7 − 1	4 − 2	5 − 2	6 − 3
6 − 5	3 − 0	6 − 2	7 − 3	6 − 5	1 − 1
4 − 4	2 − 1	4 − 0	6 − 0	6 − 6	7 − 5
3 − 1	5 − 3	1 − 0	4 − 3	5 − 0	5 − 5

How am I doing?

Accuracy
❑ I got them all right!
❑ I missed a couple.
❑ I will practice these:
(List up to 3 facts.)

Efficiency
I used these strategies:
❑ Minus Zero and
  A Number Minus Itself
❑ Count Back −1, −2, −3
❑ Count Up from bottom number
❑ Doubles Subtraction

Time
I finished in:
_____

My next goal is:
_____

Name _____   My Score _____

Test Your Skills

9 − 8	10 − 4	7 − 6	8 − 0	9 − 2	8 − 4
8 − 6	9 − 2	10 − 4	9 − 6	7 − 2	10 − 1
10 − 2	9 − 4	10 − 6	9 − 7	10 − 10	9 − 8
9 − 7	7 − 3	10 − 5	7 − 7	8 − 1	8 − 3
8 − 5	8 − 7	7 − 5	9 − 5	8 − 8	10 − 0
10 − 3	8 − 4	10 − 7	9 − 9	10 − 9	9 − 7

How am I doing?

Accuracy
❏ I got them all right!
❏ I missed a couple.
❏ I will practice these:
(List up to 3 facts.)

Efficiency
I used these strategies:
❏ Count Back −1, −2, −3
❏ Count Up from bottom number
❏ Doubles Subtraction
❏ Tens Partners Subtraction

Time
I finished in:
_____

My next goal is:
_____

Test Your Skills

9 − 3	10 − 0	8 − 5	9 − 5	8 − 7	9 − 7
10 − 6	9 − 9	10 − 2	8 − 8	10 − 4	10 − 10
7 − 7	9 − 7	10 − 3	10 − 9	10 − 5	9 − 1
9 − 4	10 − 1	8 − 6	9 − 6	9 − 2	9 − 8
7 − 6	8 − 4	7 − 2	8 − 0	7 − 4	8 − 2
7 − 5	8 − 3	9 − 6	10 − 7	7 − 3	8 − 1

How am I doing?

Accuracy
❏ I got them all right!
❏ I missed a couple.
❏ I will practice these:
   (List up to 3 facts.)

Efficiency
I used these strategies:
❏ Count Back −1, −2, −3
❏ Count Up from bottom number
❏ Doubles Subtraction
❏ Tens Partners Subtraction

Time
I finished in:

_____

My next goal is:

_____

Name _____   My Score _____

Test Your Skills

7 − 2	10 − 3	7 − 7	6 − 5	9 − 3	10 − 7
8 − 0	10 − 2	8 − 3	9 − 8	10 − 5	8 − 6
8 − 7	9 − 7	8 − 4	7 − 5	9 − 9	10 − 6
10 − 1	8 − 5	10 − 4	9 − 6	8 − 7	10 − 9
6 − 4	10 − 10	7 − 3	9 − 1	8 − 3	9 − 5
9 − 2	10 − 8	8 − 2	7 − 5	10 − 5	9 − 4

How am I doing?

Accuracy
❏ I got them all right!
❏ I missed a couple.
❏ I will practice these:
    (List up to 3 facts.)

Efficiency
I used these strategies:
❏ Count Back −1, −2, −3
❏ Count Up from bottom number
❏ Doubles Subtraction
❏ Tens Partners Subtraction

Time
I finished in:
_____

My next goal is:
_____

Name _____   My Score _____

Test Your Skills

10 − 0	12 − 2	10 − 4	11 − 6	10 − 7	12 − 9
11 − 2	10 − 5	11 − 6	10 − 8	11 − 8	12 − 3
12 − 5	12 − 7	10 − 3	11 − 11	12 − 1	11 − 9
12 − 3	10 − 1	10 − 5	12 − 7	10 − 6	12 − 5
11 − 3	12 − 6	11 − 7	11 − 9	12 − 2	12 − 4
12 − 0	12 − 8	11 − 10	12 − 9	11 − 4	11 − 8

How am I doing?

Accuracy
❏ I got them all right!
❏ I missed a couple.
❏ I will practice these:
(List up to 3 facts.)

Efficiency
I used these strategies:
❏ Count Back/Count Up
❏ Think Addition
❏ Doubles Subtraction
❏ Tens Partners Subtraction

Time
I finished in:

_____

My next goal is:

_____

Building Math Fluency • EMC 3033 • © Evan-Moor Corp.

Name _____   My Score _____

Test Your Skills

12 − 7	11 − 1	10 − 7	12 − 5	11 − 9	12 − 1

11 − 5	11 − 9	12 − 4	11 − 3	11 − 7	11 − 8

10 − 1	10 − 5	10 − 10	12 − 3	10 − 3	10 − 8

11 − 4	11 − 8	12 − 3	11 − 2	11 − 6	11 − 10

12 − 8	12 − 0	12 − 2	12 − 7	12 − 10	11 − 4

10 − 2	12 − 6	10 − 9	11 − 0	10 − 4	12 − 9

How am
I doing?

Accuracy
❏ I got them all right!
❏ I missed a couple.
❏ I will practice these:
   (List up to 3 facts.)

Efficiency
I used these strategies:
❏ Count Back/Count Up
❏ Think Addition
❏ Doubles Subtraction
❏ Tens Partners Subtraction

Time
I finished in:
_____

My next goal is:
_____

Name _____   My Score _____

Test Your Skills

13 − 2	14 − 4	13 − 6	15 − 8	13 − 10	14 − 5
14 − 7	13 − 9	15 − 4	14 − 6	15 − 7	13 − 10
14 − 2	14 − 0	14 − 1	15 − 2	15 − 0	14 − 9
13 − 13	15 − 5	13 − 7	13 − 9	14 − 7	15 − 6
14 − 8	14 − 10	15 − 9	13 − 7	15 − 15	14 − 3
13 − 12	13 − 11	15 − 3	14 − 14	13 − 5	15 − 1

How am I doing?

Accuracy
❏ I got them all right!
❏ I missed a couple.
❏ I will practice these:
(List up to 3 facts.)

Efficiency
I used these strategies:
❏ Count Back/Count Up
❏ Think Addition
❏ Minus Ten
❏ Other:

Time
I finished in:
_____
My next goal is:
_____

Name _____   My Score _____

Test Your Skills

15 − 4	15 − 8	14 − 9	13 − 7	15 − 10	15 − 6
13 − 7	14 − 4	15 − 5	13 − 3	14 − 6	13 − 9
13 − 6	15 − 11	13 − 4	13 − 8	14 − 5	15 − 12
15 − 13	15 − 9	14 − 10	13 − 10	14 − 3	15 − 7
15 − 3	13 − 11	14 − 0	13 − 1	15 − 14	15 − 1
14 − 14	15 − 0	14 − 11	13 − 2	14 − 13	13 − 8

How am I doing?

Accuracy
❏ I got them all right!
❏ I missed a couple.
❏ I will practice these:
   (List up to 3 facts.)

Efficiency
I used these strategies:
❏ Count Back/Count Up
❏ Think Addition
❏ Minus Ten
❏ Other:

Time
I finished in:
_____

My next goal is:
_____

Name _____ My Score _____

Test Your Skills

13 − 10	14 − 6	14 − 4	15 − 8	13 − 9	14 − 7
15 − 8	14 − 3	15 − 9	12 − 6	15 − 7	11 − 10
8 − 3	7 − 5	10 − 2	9 − 7	8 − 5	7 − 3
13 − 4	15 − 6	13 − 5	14 − 11	13 − 3	12 − 8
14 − 9	15 − 5	14 − 14	11 − 7	14 − 8	15 − 12
10 − 5	9 − 6	10 − 4	14 − 9	11 − 8	14 − 5

How am I doing?

Accuracy
❏ I got them all right!
❏ I missed a couple.
❏ I will practice these:
(List up to 3 facts.)

Efficiency
I used these strategies:
❏ Count Back/Count Up
❏ Think Addition
❏ Minus Ten
❏ Other:

Time
I finished in:
_____

My next goal is:
_____

Name _____   My Score _____

Test Your Skills

15 − 4	15 − 6	15 − 8	15 − 10	16 − 5	16 − 7
16 − 9	17 − 4	17 − 6	17 − 8	17 − 10	15 − 12
16 − 3	17 − 3	16 − 0	15 − 5	15 − 7	15 − 9
16 − 4	16 − 14	16 − 8	16 − 10	17 − 15	17 − 7
17 − 9	15 − 0	15 − 3	16 − 2	17 − 2	17 − 1
15 − 15	17 − 17	15 − 14	16 − 16	16 − 11	17 − 16

How am I doing?

Accuracy
❏ I got them all right!
❏ I missed a couple.
❏ I will practice these:
   (List up to 3 facts.)

Efficiency
I used these strategies:
❏ Count Back/Count Up
❏ Think Addition
❏ Minus Ten
❏ Other:

Time
I finished in:
_____

My next goal is:
_____

Name _____   My Score _____

Test Your Skills

16 − 0	15 − 7	16 − 3	15 − 9	17 − 3	15 − 5
16 − 8	17 − 5	16 − 4	17 − 7	16 − 6	16 − 10
15 − 8	16 − 15	15 − 4	16 − 7	15 − 6	15 − 10
15 − 13	17 − 2	17 − 9	17 − 11	15 − 0	16 − 2
17 − 6	17 − 10	16 − 9	15 − 15	17 − 4	17 − 8
15 − 14	16 − 16	17 − 16	15 − 2	17 − 17	16 − 11

How am
I doing?

Accuracy
❏ I got them all right!
❏ I missed a couple.
❏ I will practice these:
(List up to 3 facts.)

Efficiency
I used these strategies:
❏ Count Back/Count Up
❏ Think Addition
❏ Minus Ten
❏ Other:

Time
I finished in:
_____

My next goal is:
_____

Name _____   My Score _____

Test Your Skills

18 − 4	18 − 6	18 − 8	18 − 10	19 − 5	19 − 7
19 − 10	20 − 0	20 − 10	20 − 6	20 − 8	20 − 4
18 − 2	19 − 3	19 − 1	20 − 12	18 − 10	19 − 9
18 − 5	18 − 7	18 − 9	19 − 4	19 − 6	19 − 8
19 − 15	20 − 1	20 − 5	20 − 7	20 − 9	18 − 3
18 − 11	19 − 2	20 − 3	19 − 0	18 − 15	20 − 7

How am I doing?

Accuracy
❏ I got them all right!
❏ I missed a couple.
❏ I will practice these:
   (List up to 3 facts.)

Efficiency
I used these strategies:
❏ Count Back/Count Up
❏ Think Addition
❏ Minus Ten
❏ Other:

Time
I finished in:
_____

My next goal is:
_____

Name _____   My Score _____

Test Your Skills

19 − 3	18 − 1	20 − 2	18 − 18	19 − 4	19 − 1
20 − 1	20 − 9	20 − 7	19 − 10	18 − 3	20 − 5
20 − 20	20 − 8	20 − 6	19 − 9	20 − 10	20 − 4
18 − 6	19 − 5	18 − 10	18 − 14	19 − 7	18 − 8
19 − 2	18 − 5	19 − 10	18 − 0	20 − 7	20 − 3
18 − 17	19 − 6	19 − 17	18 − 13	19 − 19	18 − 9

How am I doing?

Accuracy
❑ I got them all right!
❑ I missed a couple.
❑ I will practice these:
(List up to 3 facts.)

Efficiency
I used these strategies:
❑ Count Back/Count Up
❑ Think Addition
❑ Minus Ten
❑ Other:

Time
I finished in:
_____

My next goal is:
_____

Name _____   My Score _____

Test Your Skills

18 − 4	17 − 5	18 − 7	19 − 4	18 − 10	19 − 5
19 − 7	20 − 20	19 − 8	20 − 1	19 − 9	20 − 5
20 − 6	15 − 13	14 − 9	20 − 10	18 − 2	19 − 3
19 − 17	20 − 3	18 − 1	18 − 5	19 − 6	17 − 16
17 − 8	16 − 16	16 − 8	19 − 7	15 − 4	14 − 6
19 − 8	13 − 11	12 − 6	11 − 5	18 − 9	20 − 2

How am I doing?

Accuracy
❏ I got them all right!
❏ I missed a couple.
❏ I will practice these:
  (List up to 3 facts.)

Efficiency
I used these strategies:
❏ Count Back/Count Up
❏ Think Addition
❏ Minus Ten
❏ Other:

Time
I finished in:
_____

My next goal is:
_____

How to Use
Facts Flashcards

Practice with flashcards can help students gain automaticity with math facts. Flashcards enable students to work at their own pace and to focus on the specific facts that they need to learn.

Prepare the Flashcards

- Reproduce the cards that students need to practice. Within each operation, the cards progress from easier to more difficult facts. Keep the cards to a manageable number; add new cards as facts are mastered.

- Students cut the cards apart and store them in an envelope or in a self-sealing plastic bag.

1 + 1	2 + 0	2 + 1	2 + 2
Addition	Addition	Addition	Addition
3 + 0	3 + 1	3 + 2	3 + 3
Addition	Addition	Addition	Addition
4 + 1	4 + 2	4 + 3	4 + 4
Addition			Addition

Tips for Practicing the Flashcards

- When students practice independently, encourage them to softly say the facts aloud to incorporate the aural modality.

- Have students practice with a partner. This is more fun and it ensures that students are computing each answer and not just looking at the answer.
If an answer is incorrect, the partner should say, for example, "No, 8 + 6 is 14." Then the answering student should repeat the equation aloud.

- Have students sort and then practice the cards by the strategies they would use to compute the answers. For example:
  Easy Facts—Plus Zero or Minus Zero; Count Up +1, +2, +3
  Doubles or Doubles Plus One
  Tens Partners
  Count Up or Count Back Subtraction

- Allow students to personalize their cards to show the strategies used to compute the answers.

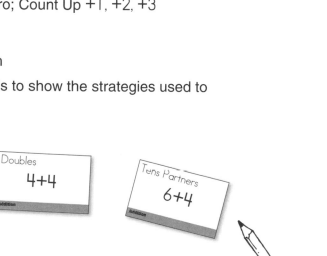

Building Math Fluency • EMC 3033 • © Evan-Moor Corp.

$2+2$	$2+1$	$2+0$	$1+1$
Addition	Addition	Addition	Addition
$3+3$	$3+2$	$3+1$	$3+0$
Addition	Addition	Addition	Addition
$4+4$	$4+3$	$4+2$	$4+1$
Addition	Addition	Addition	Addition

4

6

8

3

5

7

2

4

6

2

3

5

5 + 3	5 + 2	5 + 1	5 + 0
Addition	Addition	Addition	Addition
6 + 1	6 + 0	5 + 5	5 + 4
Addition	Addition	Addition	Addition
6 + 5	6 + 4	6 + 3	6 + 2
Addition	Addition	Addition	Addition

8

7

6

7

6

5

11

10

10

9

9

8

2

7+2	7+1	7+0	6+6
Addition	Addition	Addition	Addition

7+6	7+5	7+4	7+3
Addition	Addition	Addition	Addition

8+2	8+1	8+0	7+7
Addition	Addition	Addition	Addition

9

8

7

12

13

12

11

10

10

9

8

14

8 + 6

Addition

9 + 1

Addition

9 + 5

Addition

8 + 5

Addition

9 + 0

Addition

9 + 4

Addition

8 + 4

8 + 8

Addition

9 + 3

Addition

8 + 3

Addition

8 + 7

Addition

9 + 2

Addition

14	13	12	11
Building Math Fluency EMC 3033 • © Evan-Moor Corp.	Building Math Fluency EMC 3033 • © Evan-Moor Corp.	Building Math Fluency EMC 3033 • © Evan-Moor Corp.	Building Math Fluency EMC 3033 • © Evan-Moor Corp.
10	9	16	15
Building Math Fluency EMC 3033 • © Evan-Moor Corp.	Building Math Fluency EMC 3033 • © Evan-Moor Corp.	Building Math Fluency EMC 3033 • © Evan-Moor Corp.	Building Math Fluency EMC 3033 • © Evan-Moor Corp.
14	13	12	11
Building Math Fluency EMC 3033 • © Evan-Moor Corp.	Building Math Fluency EMC 3033 • © Evan-Moor Corp.	Building Math Fluency EMC 3033 • © Evan-Moor Corp.	Building Math Fluency EMC 3033 • © Evan-Moor Corp.

9 + 9	10 + 3	10 + 7
Addition	**Addition**	**Addition**
9 + 8	10 + 2	10 + 6
Addition	**Addition**	**Addition**
9 + 7	10 + 1	10 + 5
Addition	**Addition**	**Addition**
9 + 6	10 + 0	10 + 4
Addition	**Addition**	**Addition**

3

18

17

16

15

13

12

11

10

17

16

15

14

11 + 0	10 + 10	10 + 9
Addition		
11 + 4	11 + 3	11 + 2
Addition		
11 + 8	11 + 7	11 + 6
Addition		

10 + 8	**Addition**	11 + 1	**Addition**	11 + 5	**Addition**

11

20

19

15

14

13

19

18

18

17

12

16

12 + 2

Addition

12 + 6

Addition

13 + 1

Addition

12 + 1

Addition

12 + 5

Addition

13 + 0

Addition

12 + 0

Addition

12 + 4

Addition

12 + 8

Addition

11 + 9

Addition

12 + 3

Addition

12 + 7

Addition

14

13

12

18

17

16

14

13

20

20

15

19

$13 + 5$

Addition

$14 + 1$

Addition

$14 + 5$

Addition

$13 + 4$

Addition

$14 + 0$

Addition

$14 + 4$

Addition

$13 + 3$

Addition

$13 + 7$

Addition

$14 + 3$

Addition

$13 + 2$

Addition

$13 + 6$

Addition

$14 + 2$

Addition

18

17

16

15

15

14

20

19

19

18

17

16

	Addition		Addition	
$15 + 2$		$16 + 0$		$16 + 4$
$15 + 1$	Addition	$15 + 5$	Addition	$16 + 3$
$15 + 0$	Addition	$15 + 4$	Addition	$16 + 2$
$14 + 6$	Addition	$15 + 3$	Addition	$16 + 1$

17

Building Math Fluency
EMC 3033 • © Evan-Moor Corp.

16

Building Math Fluency
EMC 3033 • © Evan-Moor Corp.

15

Building Math Fluency
EMC 3033 • © Evan-Moor Corp.

16

Building Math Fluency
EMC 3033 • © Evan-Moor Corp.

20

Building Math Fluency
EMC 3033 • © Evan-Moor Corp.

19

Building Math Fluency
EMC 3033 • © Evan-Moor Corp.

20

Building Math Fluency
EMC 3033 • © Evan-Moor Corp.

19

Building Math Fluency
EMC 3033 • © Evan-Moor Corp.

18

Building Math Fluency
EMC 3033 • © Evan-Moor Corp.

20

Building Math Fluency
EMC 3033 • © Evan-Moor Corp.

18

Building Math Fluency
EMC 3033 • © Evan-Moor Corp.

17

Building Math Fluency
EMC 3033 • © Evan-Moor Corp.

18 + 0	17 + 2
Addition	Addition
19 + 1	19 + 0
Addition	Addition
17 + 1	17 + 0
Addition	Addition
18 + 2	18 + 1
Addition	Addition
	20 + 0
	Addition

18

Building Math Fluency
EMC 3033 • © Evan-Moor Corp.

19

Building Math Fluency
EMC 3033 • © Evan-Moor Corp.

18

Building Math Fluency
EMC 3033 • © Evan-Moor Corp.

20

Building Math Fluency
EMC 3033 • © Evan-Moor Corp.

19

Building Math Fluency
EMC 3033 • © Evan-Moor Corp.

20

Building Math Fluency
EMC 3033 • © Evan-Moor Corp.

17

Building Math Fluency
EMC 3033 • © Evan-Moor Corp.

19

Building Math Fluency
EMC 3033 • © Evan-Moor Corp.

20

Building Math Fluency
EMC 3033 • © Evan-Moor Corp.

8 − 0	5 − 0	4 − 0	1 − 0
Subtraction	Subtraction	Subtraction	Subtraction
7 − 1	3 − 1	2 − 1	10 − 0
Subtraction	Subtraction	Subtraction	Subtraction
5 − 2	4 − 2	3 − 2	10 − 1
Subtraction	Subtraction	Subtraction	Subtraction

8

5

4

1

6

2

1

10

3

2

1

9

9 − 2	8 − 2	7 − 2	6 − 2
Subtraction	Subtraction	Subtraction	Subtraction
5 − 3	4 − 3	3 − 3	10 − 2
Subtraction	Subtraction	Subtraction	Subtraction
9 − 3	8 − 3	7 − 3	6 − 3
Subtraction	Subtraction	Subtraction	Subtraction

7

6

4

6

5

4

2

1

0

8

5

3

7 − 4

Subtraction

5 − 5

Subtraction

9 − 5

Subtraction

6 − 4

Subtraction

10 − 4

Subtraction

8 − 5

Subtraction

5 − 4

Subtraction

9 − 4

Subtraction

7 − 5

Subtraction

10 − 3

Subtraction

8 − 4

Subtraction

6 − 5

Subtraction

3

2

7

0

6

5

4

3

2

4

1

9 – 6

Subtraction

10 – 7

Subtraction

10 – 10

Subtraction

8 – 6

Subtraction

9 – 7

Subtraction

10 – 9

Subtraction

7 – 6

Subtraction

8 – 7

Subtraction

10 – 8

Subtraction

10 – 5

Subtraction

10 – 6

Subtraction

9 – 8

Subtraction

3

2

1

5

3

2

1

4

0

1

2

1

$12 - 2$

$13 - 4$

$17 - 4$

Subtraction

Subtraction

Subtraction

$11 - 2$

$12 - 4$

$16 - 4$

Subtraction

Subtraction

Subtraction

$20 - 1$

$11 - 4$

$15 - 4$

Subtraction

Subtraction

Subtraction

$20 - 0$

$13 - 2$

$14 - 4$

Subtraction

Subtraction

Subtraction

10

9

19

9

8

7

20

13

12

11

11

10

11 − 5	15 − 5	19 − 5
Subtraction	Subtraction	Subtraction
20 − 4	14 − 5	18 − 5
Subtraction	Subtraction	Subtraction
19 − 4	13 − 5	17 − 5
Subtraction	Subtraction	Subtraction
18 − 4	12 − 5	16 − 5
Subtraction	Subtraction	Subtraction

6

16

15

14

10

9

8

7

14

13

12

11

13 − 6	12 − 6	11 − 6	20 − 5
Subtraction	**Subtraction**	**Subtraction**	**Subtraction**
17 − 6	16 − 6	15 − 6	14 − 6
Subtraction	**Subtraction**	**Subtraction**	**Subtraction**
11 − 7	20 − 6	19 − 6	18 − 6
Subtraction	**Subtraction**	**Subtraction**	**Subtraction**

7

6

5

11

10

9

8

4

14

13

15

12

$15 - 7$	$19 - 7$	$13 - 8$
Subtraction	Subtraction	Subtraction
$14 - 7$	$18 - 7$	$12 - 8$
Subtraction	Subtraction	Subtraction
$13 - 7$	$17 - 7$	$11 - 8$
Subtraction	Subtraction	Subtraction
$12 - 7$	$16 - 7$	$20 - 7$
Subtraction	Subtraction	Subtraction

8

7

6

12

11

10

5

4

3

5

9

13

Subtraction

$17 - 8$

$11 - 9$

Subtraction

$15 - 9$

Subtraction

$16 - 8$

Subtraction

$20 - 8$

Subtraction

$14 - 9$

Subtraction

$15 - 8$

$19 - 8$

Subtraction

$13 - 9$

Subtraction

$14 - 8$

Subtraction

$18 - 8$

Subtraction

$12 - 9$

Subtraction

9

8

7

6

2

12

11

10

6

5

4

3

19 − 9	13 − 10	17 − 10
Subtraction	Subtraction	Subtraction
18 − 9	12 − 10	16 − 10
Subtraction	Subtraction	Subtraction
17 − 9	11 − 10	15 − 10
Subtraction	Subtraction	Subtraction
16 − 9	20 − 9	14 − 10
Subtraction	Subtraction	Subtraction

10

9

8

7

3

2

1

11

7

6

5

4

Answer Key

Page 8

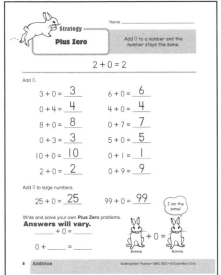

Page 9

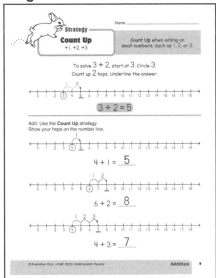

Page 10

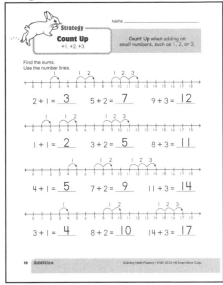

Page 11

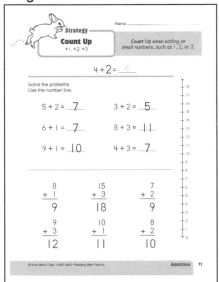

Page 12

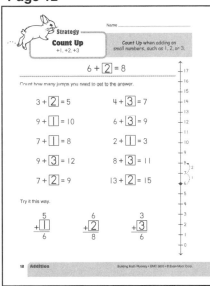

Page 13

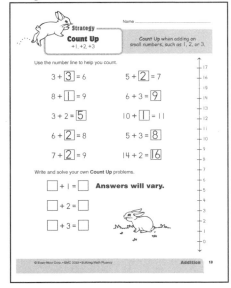

Page 14

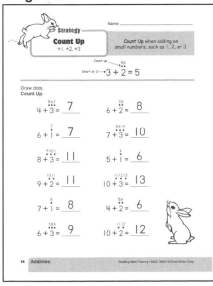

Page 15

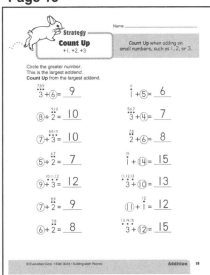

Page 16

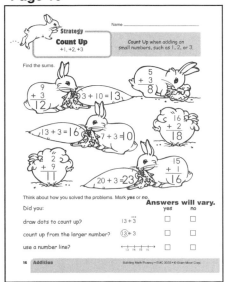

Page 17

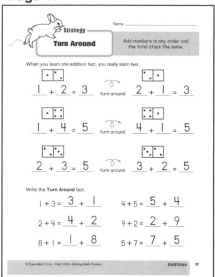

Turn Around — Add numbers in any order and the total stays the same.

When you learn one addition fact, you really learn two.

$1 + 2 = 3$ turn around $2 + 1 = 3$

$1 + 4 = 5$ turn around $4 + 1 = 5$

$2 + 3 = 5$ turn around $3 + 2 = 5$

Write the Turn Around fact.

$1 + 3 = 3 + 1$ $4 + 5 = 5 + 4$

$2 + 4 = 4 + 2$ $9 + 2 = 2 + 9$

$8 + 1 = 1 + 8$ $5 + 7 = 7 + 5$

Page 18

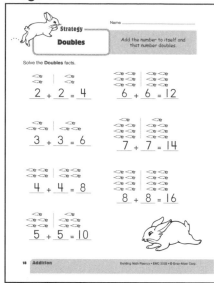

Doubles — Add the number to itself and that number doubles.

Solve the Doubles facts.

$2 + 2 = 4$ $6 + 6 = 12$

$3 + 3 = 6$ $7 + 7 = 14$

$4 + 4 = 8$ $8 + 8 = 16$

$5 + 5 = 10$

Page 19

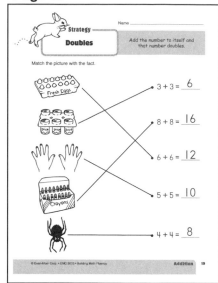

Doubles — Add the number to itself and that number doubles.

Match the picture with the fact.

$3 + 3 = 6$

$8 + 8 = 16$

$6 + 6 = 12$

$5 + 5 = 10$

$4 + 4 = 8$

Page 20

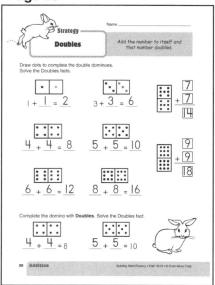

Doubles — Add the number to itself and that number doubles.

Draw dots to complete the double dominoes. Solve the Doubles facts.

$1 + 1 = 2$ $3 + 3 = 6$ $\frac{7 + 7}{14}$

$4 + 4 = 8$ $5 + 5 = 10$ $\frac{9 + 9}{18}$

$6 + 6 = 12$ $8 + 8 = 16$

Complete the domino with Doubles. Solve the Doubles fact.

$4 + 4 = 8$ $5 + 5 = 10$

Page 21

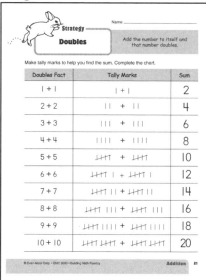

Doubles — Add the number to itself and that number doubles.

Make tally marks to help you find the sum. Complete the chart.

Doubles Fact	Tally Marks	Sum
1 + 1	I + I	2
2 + 2	II + II	4
3 + 3	III + III	6
4 + 4	IIII + IIII	8
5 + 5	ЖЖ + ЖЖ	10
6 + 6	ЖЖ I + ЖЖ I	12
7 + 7	ЖЖ II + ЖЖ II	14
8 + 8	ЖЖ III + ЖЖ III	16
9 + 9	ЖЖ IIII + ЖЖ IIII	18
10 + 10	ЖЖ ЖЖ + ЖЖ ЖЖ	20

Page 22

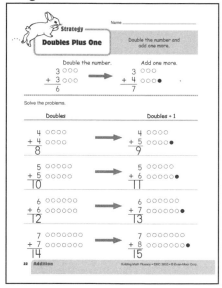

Doubles Plus One — Double the number and add one more.

Double the number.   Add one more.

$\frac{3}{+3}{6}$ → $\frac{3}{+4}{7}$

Solve the problems.

Doubles   Doubles + 1

$\frac{4}{+4}{8}$ → $\frac{4}{+5}{9}$

$\frac{5}{+5}{10}$ → $\frac{5}{+6}{11}$

$\frac{6}{+6}{12}$ → $\frac{6}{+7}{13}$

$\frac{7}{+7}{14}$ → $\frac{7}{+8}{15}$

Page 23

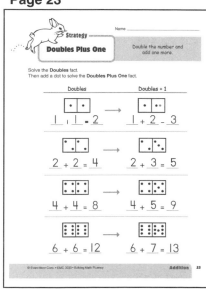

Doubles Plus One — Double the number and add one more.

Solve the Doubles fact. Then add a dot to solve the Doubles Plus One fact.

Doubles   Doubles + 1

$1 + 1 = 2$ → $1 + 2 = 3$

$2 + 2 = 4$ → $2 + 3 = 5$

$4 + 4 = 8$ → $4 + 5 = 9$

$6 + 6 = 12$ → $6 + 7 = 13$

Page 24

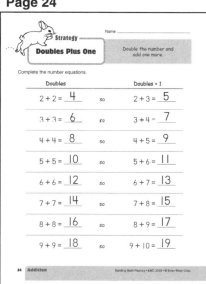

Doubles Plus One — Double the number and add one more.

Complete the number equations.

Doubles   Doubles + 1

$2 + 2 = 4$ so $2 + 3 = 5$

$3 + 3 = 6$ so $3 + 4 = 7$

$4 + 4 = 8$ so $4 + 5 = 9$

$5 + 5 = 10$ so $5 + 6 = 11$

$6 + 6 = 12$ so $6 + 7 = 13$

$7 + 7 = 14$ so $7 + 8 = 15$

$8 + 8 = 16$ so $8 + 9 = 17$

$9 + 9 = 18$ so $9 + 10 = 19$

Page 25

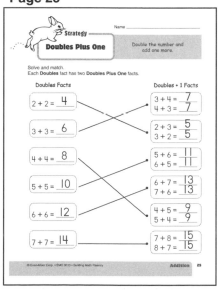

Doubles Plus One — Double the number and add one more.

Solve and match. Each Doubles fact has two Doubles Plus One facts.

Doubles Facts   Doubles + 1 Facts

$2 + 2 = 4$ $3 + 4 = 7$ / $4 + 3 = 7$

$3 + 3 = 6$ $2 + 3 = 5$ / $3 + 2 = 5$

$4 + 4 = 8$ $5 + 6 = 11$ / $6 + 5 = 11$

$5 + 5 = 10$ $6 + 7 = 13$ / $7 + 6 = 13$

$6 + 6 = 12$ $4 + 5 = 9$ / $5 + 4 = 9$

$7 + 7 = 14$ $7 + 8 = 15$ / $8 + 7 = 15$

Page 26

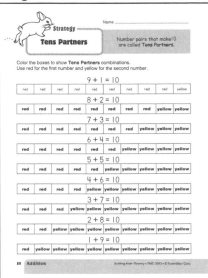

Page 27

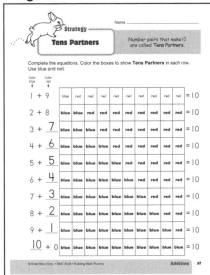

Page 28

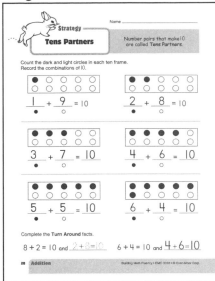

Page 29

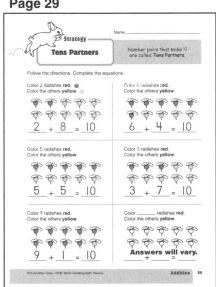

Page 30

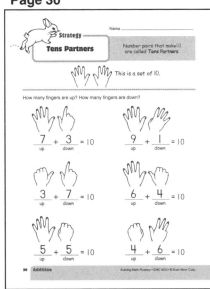

Page 31

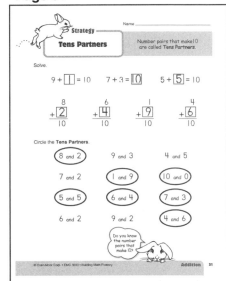

Page 32

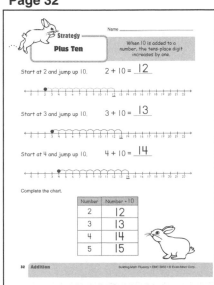

Page 33

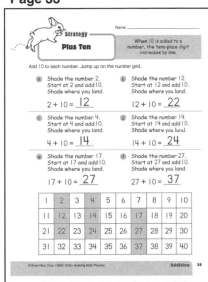

Page 34

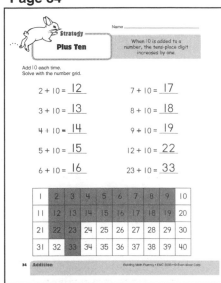

Page 35

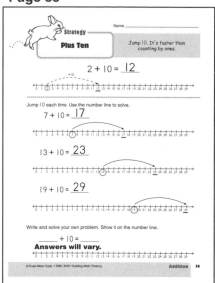

Strategy — Plus Ten

Jump 10. It's faster than counting by ones.

$2 + 10 = 12$

Jump 10 each time. Use the number line to solve.

$7 + 10 = 17$

$13 + 10 = 23$

$19 + 10 = 29$

Write and solve your own problem. Show it on the number line.

____ + 10 = ____

Answers will vary.

Page 36

Strategy — Plus Ten

When 10 is added to a number, the tens-place digit increases by one.

Add 10 to each number. Fill in the chart.

Number	Number + 10	Number	Number + 10
3	13	15	25
4	14	16	26
5	15	17	27
6	16	18	28
7	17	19	29
8	18	20	30
9	19	30	40
10	20	40	50
11	21	50	60
12	22	60	70
13	23	70	80
14	24	80	90

Note: You may want to provide a number grid or number line to help students complete the chart.

Page 37

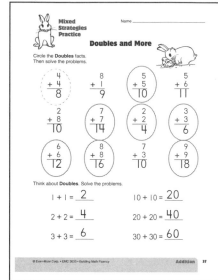

Mixed Strategies Practice — Doubles and More

Circle the **Doubles** facts. Then solve the problems.

$4 + 4 = 8$ $8 + 1 = 9$ $5 + 5 = 10$ $5 + 6 = 11$

$2 + 8 = 10$ $7 + 7 = 14$ $2 + 2 = 4$ $3 + 3 = 6$

$6 + 6 = 12$ $8 + 8 = 16$ $7 + 3 = 10$ $9 + 9 = 18$

Think about **Doubles**. Solve the problems.

$1 + 1 = 2$ $10 + 10 = 20$

$2 + 2 = 4$ $20 + 20 = 40$

$3 + 3 = 6$ $30 + 30 = 60$

Page 38

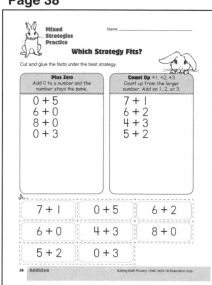

Mixed Strategies Practice — Which Strategy Fits?

Cut and glue the facts under the best strategy.

Plus Zero — Add 0 to a number and the number stays the same.
$0 + 5$
$6 + 0$
$8 + 0$
$0 + 3$

Count Up +1, +2, +3 — Count up from the larger number. Add on 1, 2, or 3.
$7 + 1$
$6 + 2$
$4 + 3$
$5 + 2$

$7 + 1$ $0 + 5$ $6 + 2$
$6 + 0$ $4 + 3$ $8 + 0$
$5 + 2$ $0 + 3$

Page 39

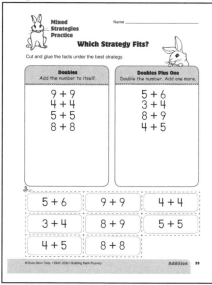

Mixed Strategies Practice — Which Strategy Fits?

Cut and glue the facts under the best strategy.

Doubles — Add the number to itself.
$9 + 9$
$4 + 4$
$5 + 5$
$8 + 8$

Doubles Plus One — Double the number. Add one more.
$5 + 6$
$3 + 4$
$8 + 9$
$4 + 5$

$5 + 6$ $9 + 9$ $4 + 4$
$3 + 4$ $8 + 9$ $5 + 5$
$4 + 5$ $8 + 8$

Page 40

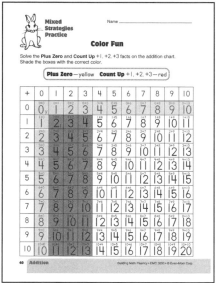

Mixed Strategies Practice — Color Fun

Solve the **Plus Zero** and **Count Up** +1, +2, +3 facts on the addition chart. Shade the boxes with the correct color.

Plus Zero — yellow   **Count Up** +1, +2, +3 — red

Page 41

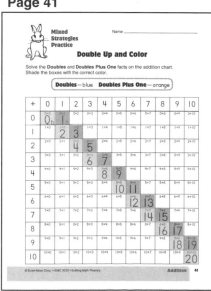

Mixed Strategies Practice — Double Up and Color

Solve the **Doubles** and **Doubles Plus One** facts on the addition chart. Shade the boxes with the correct color.

Doubles — blue   **Doubles Plus One** — orange

Page 42

Mixed Strategies Practice — It's a Mystery

Solve the **Tens Partners** and **Plus Ten** facts on the addition chart. Shade the boxes with the correct color.

Tens Partners — red   **Plus Ten** — blue

Page 43

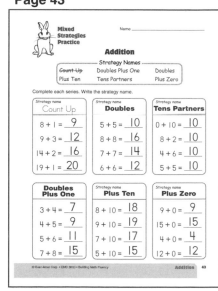

Mixed Strategies Practice — Addition

Strategy Names: Count Up, Doubles Plus One, Doubles, Plus Ten, Tens Partners, Plus Zero

Complete each series. Write the strategy name.

Count Up
$8 + 1 = 9$
$9 + 3 = 12$
$14 + 2 = 16$
$19 + 1 = 20$

Doubles
$5 + 5 = 10$
$8 + 8 = 16$
$7 + 7 = 14$
$6 + 6 = 12$

Tens Partners
$0 + 10 = 10$
$8 + 2 = 10$
$4 + 6 = 10$
$5 + 5 = 10$

Doubles Plus One
$3 + 4 = 7$
$4 + 5 = 9$
$5 + 6 = 11$
$7 + 8 = 15$

Plus Ten
$8 + 10 = 18$
$9 + 10 = 19$
$7 + 10 = 17$
$5 + 10 = 15$

Plus Zero
$9 + 0 = 9$
$15 + 0 = 15$
$4 + 0 = 4$
$12 + 0 = 12$

Page 44

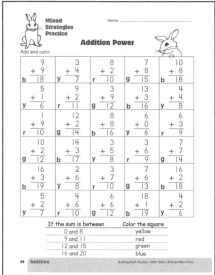

Page 47

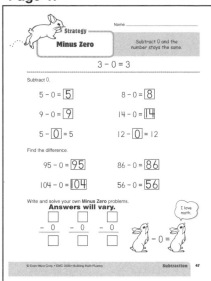

Page 48

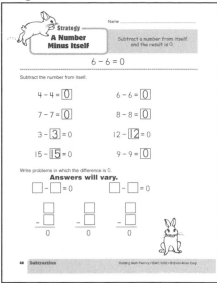

Page 49

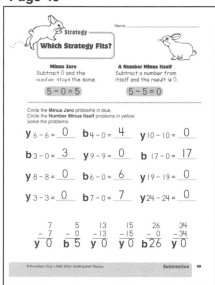

Page 50

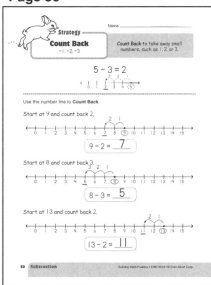

Page 51

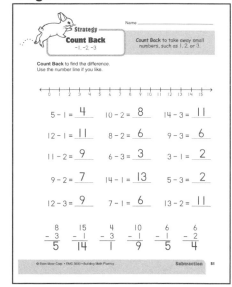

Page 52

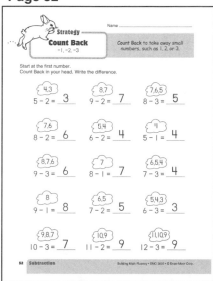

Page 53

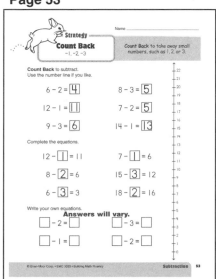

Page 54

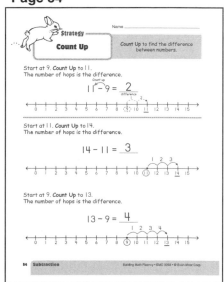

Page 55

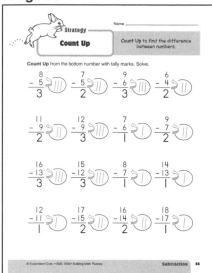

Page 56

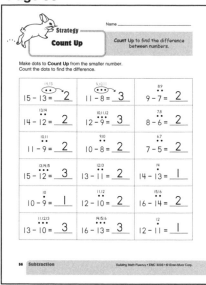

Page 57

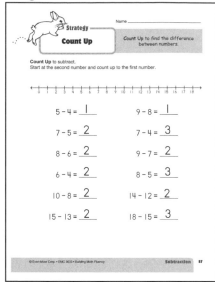

Page 58

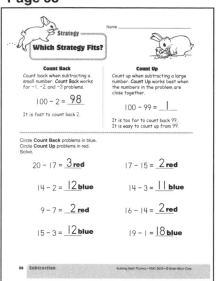

Page 59

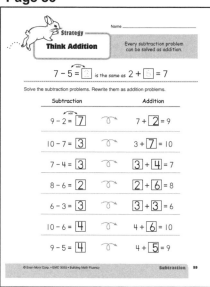

Page 60

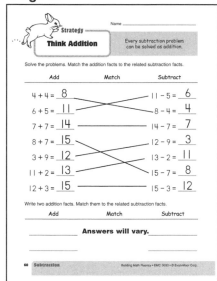

Page 61

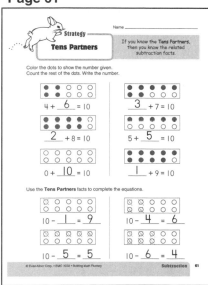

Page 62

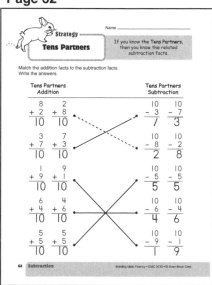

Page 63

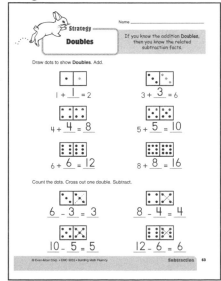

Page 64

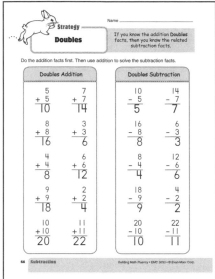

Page 65

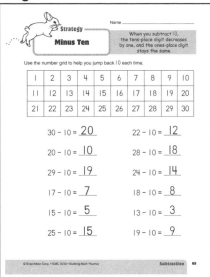

Page 66

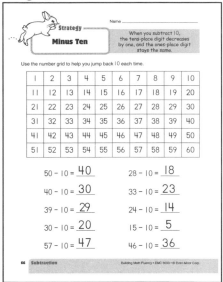

Page 67

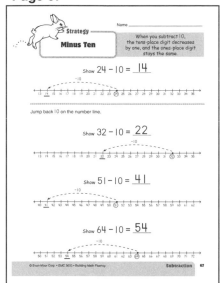

Page 68

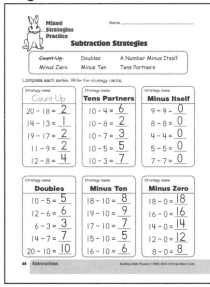

Page 69

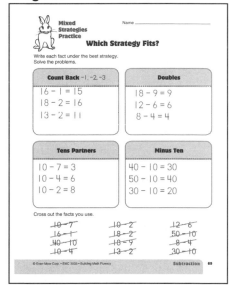

Page 70

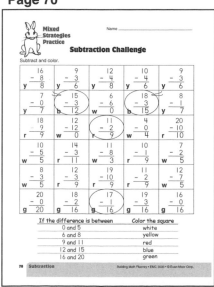

Page 71

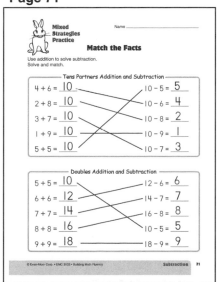

Page 72

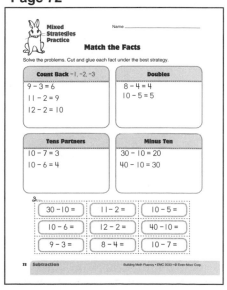

Page 73

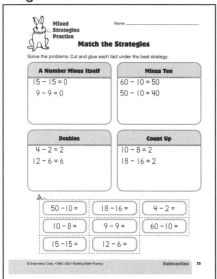

Page 74

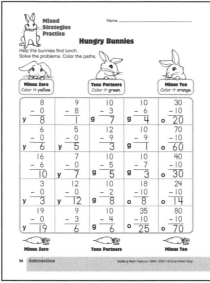

Page 75

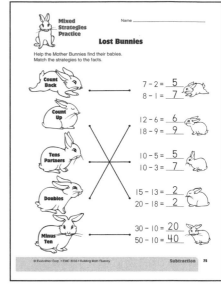

Page 79

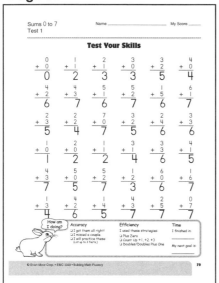

Page 80

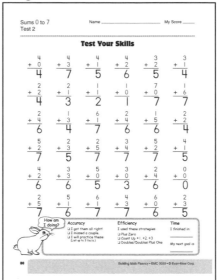

Page 81

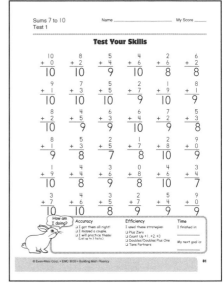

Page 82

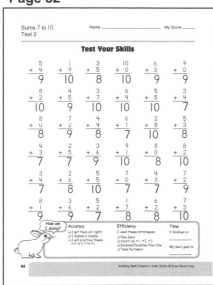

Page 83

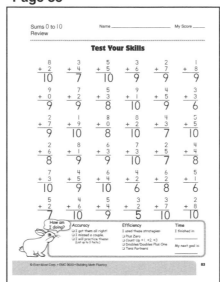

Page 84

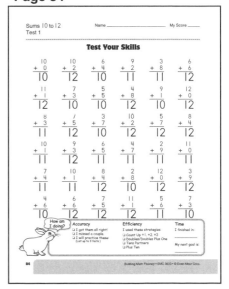

Building Math Fluency • EMC 3033 • © Evan-Moor Corp.

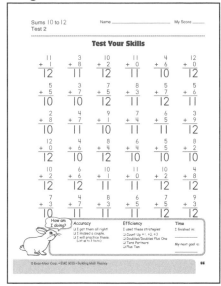

Sums 10 to 12 — Test 2 — Test Your Skills

```
11+1=12   3+8=11   10+2=12   11+0=11   4+6=10   12+0=12
 5+5=10   3+7=10    7+5=12    8+3=11   5+7=12    5+6=11
 2+8=10   4+7=11    9+1=10    7+4=11   6+5=11    3+9=12
12+0=12   4+6=10    8+4=12    6+4=10   5+5=10    8+2=10
10+2=12   6+5=11   10+1=11   11+0=11  10+2=12    4+8=12
 7+3=10   4+7=11    8+3=11    6+5=11   7+4=11    9+3=12
```

How am I doing? — Accuracy: ☐ I got them all right! ☐ I missed a couple. ☐ I will practice these: (List up to 3 facts.) — Efficiency: I used these strategies: ☐ Count Up +1, +2, +3 ☐ Doubles/Doubles Plus One ☐ Tens Partners ☐ Plus Ten — Time: I finished in: ___ — My next goal is: ___

Sums 13 to 15 — Test 1 — Test Your Skills

```
13+0=13   8+5=13   9+4=13   10+5=15   6+7=13   14+1=15
13+1=14  12+3=15   9+5=14   15+0=15  11+2=13   10+4=14
 8+6=14   4+9=13  11+3=14   12+2=14  11+4=15   12+1=13
10+4=14  12+3=15   8+7=15   15+0=15  13+1=14   13+2=15
10+3=13  12+2=14  11+2=13   12+1=13  10+5=15    8+6=14
 9+6=15   7+8=15   5+8=13    7+7=14   4+9=13     7+6=13
```

How am I doing? (same skill-check box as above)

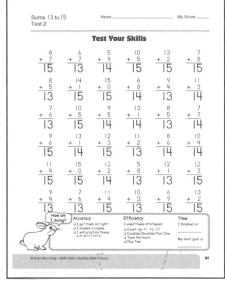

Sums 13 to 15 — Test 2 — Test Your Skills

```
 8+7=15   6+7=13   5+9=14   10+5=15  13+2=15    7+8=15
 8+5=13  14+1=15  15+0=15    6+8=14   9+4=13   11+3=14
 8+5=13  10+5=15   9+5=14   13+0=13   8+7=15    7+7=14
 9+4=13  13+1=14  12+3=15   11+2=13   8+6=14   10+4=14
11+4=15  15+0=15  12+2=14    5+8=13  12+1=13   12+3=15
 9+4=13   7+6=13  11+4=15   10+3=13   6+9=15   13+2=15
```

How am I doing? (same skill-check box as above)

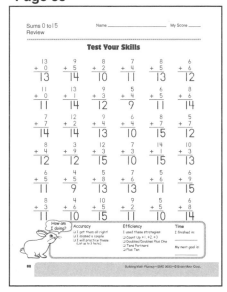

Sums 0 to 15 — Review — Test Your Skills

```
13+0=13   9+5=14   8+2=10   7+4=11   8+5=13   6+6=12
11+0=11  13+1=14   9+3=12   5+4=9    6+5=11   8+6=14
 7+7=14  12+2=14   9+4=13   6+4=10   8+7=15   5+7=12
 8+4=12   3+9=12  12+3=15   7+3=10  14+1=15  10+3=13
 6+5=11   4+5=9    5+8=13   7+6=13   5+6=11   6+9=15
 8+3=11   4+6=10  10+5=15   9+1=10   5+5=10   6+8=14
```

How am I doing? (same skill-check box as above)

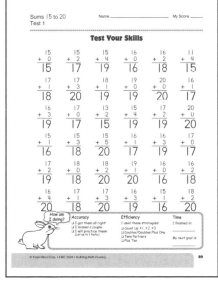

Sums 15 to 20 — Test 1 — Test Your Skills

```
15+0=15  15+2=17  15+4=19  16+0=16  16+2=18  11+4=15
17+1=18  17+3=20  18+1=19  19+0=19  20+0=20  16+1=17
16+3=19  17+0=17  13+2=15  15+4=19  17+2=19  20+0=20
15+1=16  15+3=18  15+5=20  16+1=17  16+3=19  17+0=17
17+2=19  16+2=18  18+2=20  20+0=20  16+0=16  16+2=18
16+4=20  17+1=18  17+3=20  16+0=16  15+2=17  18+2=20
```

How am I doing? (same skill-check box as above)

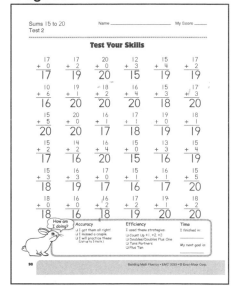

Sums 15 to 20 — Test 2 — Test Your Skills

```
17+0=17  17+2=19  20+0=20  12+3=15  15+4=19  17+2=19
10+6=16  19+1=20  18+2=20  16+4=20  15+3=18  17+3=20
15+5=20  20+0=20  16+1=17  17+1=18  19+0=19  18+1=19
15+2=17  14+2=16  16+4=20  15+0=15  13+6=19  15+4=19
15+3=18  16+3=19  17+0=17  15+1=16  16+1=17  15+5=20
18+0=18  16+0=16  16+2=18  17+2=19  19+1=20  18+0=18
```

How am I doing? (same skill-check box as above)

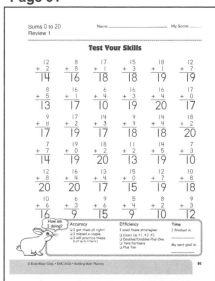

Sums 0 to 20 — Review 1 — Test Your Skills

```
12+2=14   8+8=16  17+1=18  15+3=18  18+1=19  12+7=19
 8+5=13  16+1=17   6+4=10  16+3=19  16+4=20  17+0=17
 9+8=17  17+2=19  14+3=17   9+9=18  14+4=18  18+2=20
 7+7=14  19+0=19  18+2=20  11+2=13  14+5=19   7+3=10
12+8=20  16+4=20  13+4=17  15+0=15  12+7=19  10+8=18
10+6=16   6+3=9    9+6=15   5+4=9    8+2=10    9+3=12
```

How am I doing? (same skill-check box as above)

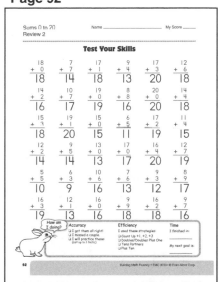

Sums 0 to 20 — Review 2 — Test Your Skills

```
18+0=18   7+7=14  17+1=18   9+4=13  17+3=20  12+6=18
14+2=16  12+7=19  19+0=19   8+8=16  20+0=20  14+4=18
15+3=18  11+9=20  15+0=15   6+5=11  17+2=19  11+4=15
12+2=14   9+5=14  10+3=13  17+0=17  16+4=20  12+7=19
 5+5=10   6+3=9   10+6=16   6+7=13   9+3=12   8+9=17
19+0=19   8+1=9    9+6=15   6+9=15   9+7=16   7+9=16
```

How am I doing? (same skill-check box as above)

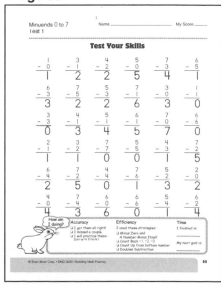

Minuends 0 to 7 — Test 1 — Test Your Skills

```
1-0=1   3-1=2   4-2=2   5-0=5   7-3=4   6-5=1
6-3=3   7-5=2   5-3=2   7-1=6   3-0=3   3-3=0
3-3=0   4-1=3   5-1=4   6-1=5   7-0=7   6-6=0
2-1=1   3-3=0   7-7=0   5-4=1   5-3=2   7-2=5
6-4=2   7-4=3   5-0=5   6-3=3   4-1=3   5-2=3
4-0=4   7-6=1   6-6=0   6-4=2   6-2=4   6-5=1
```

How am I doing? — Accuracy: ☐ I got them all right! ☐ I missed a couple. ☐ I will practice these: (List up to 3 facts.) — Efficiency: I used these strategies: ☐ Minus Zero and A Number Minus Itself ☐ Count Up from bottom number ☐ Doubles Subtraction — Time: I finished in: ___ — My next goal is: ___

Page 94
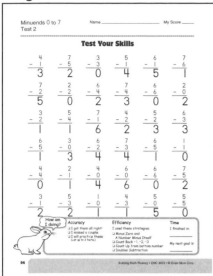

Page 95
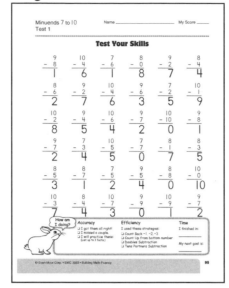

Page 96
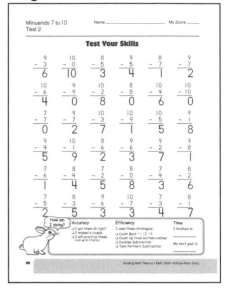

Page 97
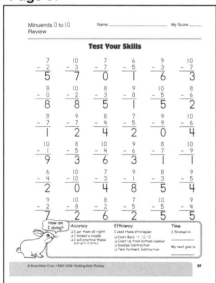

Page 98
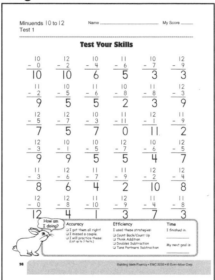

Page 99

Page 100
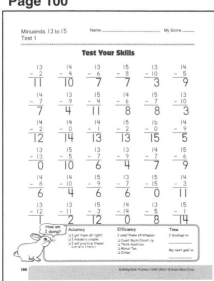

Page 101
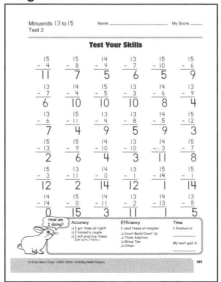

Page 102
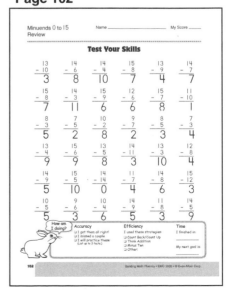

Page 103

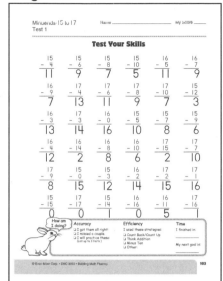

Page 104

Page 105

Page 106

Page 107